AN INTRODUCTION TO EXTENSION EDUCATION

An Introduction to Extension Education

(SECOND EDITION)

S.V. SUPE
M.A. (Eco.), M.Sc. (Agri), Ph.D.

OXFORD & IBH PUBLISHING CO. PVT. LTD.
New Delhi

AN INTRODUCTION TO EXTENSION EDUCATION

Oxford & IBH Publishing Company Pvt. Ltd.
113-B ShahpurJat
Asian Games Village Side
New Delhi 110 049, India

Fax: (011) 4151 7559
Email: oxford@oxford-ibh.in

Last Reprint 2017

ISBN 978-81-204-1178-4

Printed at Chaman Enterprises, New Delhi.

12-F7-05

Preface to the Second Edition

The wide acceptability of this book by extension educators and students is gratifying. Longstanding demand for alteration and addition to this book will be fulfilled by this second edition. I felt it would be worthwhile to mention some misconceptions about extension, innovation, decision process, salient features and problems of extension organisation, environment, culture and social interaction. This effort was to ensure that the contents were in harmony with the curricular requirement of the students and help them in understanding the basic issues involved in performing field work. I believe this edition of the book will greatly benefit not only the wide range of extension workers, but also every person interested in promoting rural development programmes through educational means.

S.V. SUPE

Preface to the First Edition

Many people in technologically less advanced areas are reluctant or unable to accept change. To overcome this problem various programmes of rural development are initiated. However, in most of these programmes there is an absence of understanding about the concepts, philosophy, objectives and method of working with the rural people among the field level workers. Many times it comes as a surprise to them that in spite of providing the best technical staff in these programmes, they are not making much headway. Close evaluation of these programmes will show the absence of the extension educator who would have taken care of the factors that determine the motivations and resistances in change. Increasing recognition needs to be given to human factors in technological development. The staff who work in these programmes do better if they understand something about extension education.

As the title of the book indicates it is an introduction of extension education for the students enrolled in introductory extension education courses. Extension education courses have been introduced in most of the agricultural universities for students of agriculture, veterinary sciences, home science, dairy, engineering and fisheries. It is hoped that this book will be helpful to these students in a preliminary understanding of this subject. This understanding is expected to help them in future while working in rural development programmes. The book will also be useful for the gramsevak training centres, agricultural schools and other extension training institutions as well as to all categories of field extension personnel.

In the preparation of this book, benefit of the valuable work of outstanding scholars and other publications was taken I acknowledge with thanks this valuable debt and welcome any suggestions for the improvement of this book.

I am grateful to Dr. S.N. Singh, Communication Specialist, Indian Agricultural Research Institute, New Delhi; Mr. S.R. Chopde, former Director of Agriculture, Maharashtra State, Pune; Dr. K.R. Thakare, Vice-Chancellor, Punjabrao Krishi Vidyapeeth, Akola; Dr. P.L. Ganorkar, Reader in Agricultural Extension, Punjabrao Krishi Vidyapeeth Akola and others, who inspired me for writing this book. My thanks are also due to Mr. K.W. Waghdhare for the primary editing of the manuscript and for artwork. Lastly, to my wife and children for their patience, love and support during the writing of this book.

S.V. SUPE

Contents

CHAPTER 1

Extension Education

Towards the beginning of this century there was a feeling among eminent social workers that rural life was fast deteriorating due to several factors. These social workers planned several experiments in rural reconstruction to rebuild rural life. The experiments proved beneficial in the area where they were undertaken. A close scrutiny of these efforts provides an insight into the background of the extension education approach adopted in the country.

EARLY EFFORTS IN RURAL RECONSTRUCTION

Gurgaon Attempt

This was organised by F.L. Bryne, Collector of Gurgaon district in Punjab in 1920. He was prompted by the poverty and misery of the people. In the project, emphasis was laid on increasing farm yields, curtailing expenditure on social and religious functions, improving health standards and organising welfare programmes. Village guides were appointed in villages and they made extensive use of films, folk songs, dramas etc., to approach the people. Due to inherent defects in the project it could not make much headway. The project could not develop leadership in the villages that would continue work when the village guides had left the villages. The village people were never made party to the programme planned for them. Most of the work was done by exercising authority over the people rather than by obtaining voluntary participation from them.

Sevagram Attempt

It was started under the guidance of Mahatma Gandhi in

1920. The objectives of the project were to provide service to the underprivileged, achieving self dependency and providing basic education to the people. The main activities of the project were, organisation of training centres for cottage industries, prohibition, removal of untouchability, stressing women's education and basic education and preaching and practising communal unity. Very high personal standards were set in the project which were difficult for the common man to reach and therefore, the project could not provide the expected results.

Shriniketan Attempt

Rabindranath Tagore, in collaboration with Elmhirst, started this project in 1921 in Bengal. The aim of the project was to win the friendship of the villagers and to make an honest effort to assist them in solving their most pressing problems. The idea was also to develop the people's resources and their credit and to teach them better methods of growing crops, vegetables and keeping livestock. It also aimed to encourage the villagers to learn and practise arts and crafts and to bring home to them the benefits of associated life, mutual aid and common endeavour. The project could not make much headway due to lack of funds to finance the expanded activities. Comparatively less educative work was planned for women in villages. There was a tendency towards gradual urbanisation and centralisation. The project was idealistic and the practical aspect of the project was rather neglected.

Martandum Attempt

This project was started by Hatch in Travancore state in 1921 under the auspices of the Y.M.C.A. The objective of the project was to bring about a complete upward development towards a more abundant life for rural people in spiritual, mental, physical, social and economic fields. The working principles of the project were self-help with expert guidance, training persons to improve their performance, making people conscious of their wants and needs and organising reconstruction programmes to include the poorest. The main shortcomings of the project were inadequate funds and government help. The activities were mainly organised at Martandum and the village workers did not stay in villages. The religious bias of the institution was also a major hindrance in its activities.

Etawah Attempt

This project was organised by the American architect Albert Mayer in 1948. The objective of the project was to see the extent of improvement possible in production, social improvement, self reliance and cooperation in an average district and to see how quickly results could be obtained in the aforementioned aspects. It was also intended to see whether the results obtained could be permanent and introduceable elsewhere. The activities were organised with the help of trained village level workers located in the villages. Cooperation of other departments and agencies was enlisted. The demonstration method was used to convey new ideas. The project proved to be successful and on a similar pattern, extension organisation was organised in India.

In addition to the foregoing, some projects were also undertaken at Baroda, Madras, Nilokheri and Faridabad which may be mentioned in this context. The Grow More Food Enquiry Committee (1952) finally observed that all aspects of rural life were interrelated and that while planning for one aspect, other aspects of rural life could not be ignored. When particular problems might call for special attention, the plans for them should form parts of and be integrated with those for achieving the wider aims. The recommendations of this committee were responsible to a very large extent in shaping the extension approach in India.

Based on the recommendations of the Grow More Food Enquiry Committee, 55 community projects spread over the country were taken up in 1952. Afterwards the entire country was covered with development blocks and a countrywide extension organisation was established.

In the earlier days rural development was considered synonymous with community development in which the need for institutional framework to provide production facilities and basic amenities to the rural population was emphasised. Later developments led to the creation of peoples institutions for the all-round development of village communities in which democratic decentralisation was implied. Rural development was also equated with the development of agriculture and allied sectors in the rural economy. Of late, rural development has come to include transformation of social and economic structures, institutions, relationships and processes in a particular area. It conceives the goals of rural development, not as agricultural and economic growth but as a balanced social and economic development, with emphasis on equitable distribution as well as the creation of benefits. The programmes of rural development include the generation of new employment, equitable distribution of income, widespread improvement in health, nutrition and housing. It also provides opportunities for all rural people to educate and participate in decisions and actions that affect their lives.

Rural development is the result of many interacting forces and education is one of them. The educational needs for rural development are numerous and diverse but they can be usefully grouped under four main headings.

1) General or basic education: It is designed for providing literacy, an elementary understanding of science and one's environment (primary education).

2) Family improvement education: It is designed primarily to impart knowledge, skills and attitudes useful in improving the quality of family life on subjects such as health and nutrition, home making and child care, home repairs and improvements, family planning, etc.

3) Community improvement education: It is designed to strengthen local and national institutions and processes through instructions in such matters as local and national government, cooperatives, community projects, etc.

4) Occupational education: It is designed to develop particular knowledge and skills associated with various economic activities and useful in making a living.

METHODS OF EDUCATION

Rural areas have relatively poor educational resources to meet the diverse needs mentioned earlier. Education should be conceived as a lifelong process of learning. The individual learns by three methods, namely, informal education, formal education and non-formal education. The informal education is the lifelong process by which every person acquires knowledge, skills, attitudes and insights from daily experiences and exposure to environment—at home, at work, at play, from friends, from travel, reading newspapers and books or by listening to radio, viewing films or television.

Formal education is a highly institutionalised, chronologically graded and hierarchically structured education system starting from primary school and reaching to university education.

Non-formal education is any organised, systematic, educational activity carried on outside the framework of the formal system to provide selected types of learning to particular sub-groups in the population including adults as well as children. It includes agricultural extension and farmers' training programmes, adult literacy programmes, occupational skill training given outside the formal system, youth clubs with substantial educational purposes and various community programmes of instruction in health, nutrition, family planning, cooperatives and the like.

General or basic education is mostly imparted by formal education methods to children and youths by established educational institutions. The remaining three types of education are the concern of the extension workers. Different welfare programmes are organised for this purpose and education is imparted through informal and non-formal methods. This is the main area of extension education.

EXTENSION EDUCATION

Extension education is education for rural people outside the regularly organised schools and class rooms for bringing out social and cultural development. Extension means to extend, to spread or to disseminate useful information and ideas to rural people outside the regularly organised schools and class rooms. Education is the production of desirable changes in human behaviour. These changes are brought out in the social and cultural aspects of human life. The term social means anything related to human beings. Extension education tries to develop the social behaviour of the people, their different social groups and the intra- and interrelationship of these social groups. It also tries to bring out cultural development. The term culture means the socially standardised ways of feeling, thinking and acting which an individual acquires as a member of the society. The behaviour of the individual is influenced, controlled and directed by culture. The culture may be material (e.g., machines, tables, chairs, etc.) or non-material (e.g., ways of thinking, values, feelings, etc.). With changes in time and environment the patterns of culture undergo change. Sometimes one aspect of culture undergoes rapid change (may be housing or communication) leaving other aspects behind and thereby creating a cultural lag. A cultural lag occurs when technological and material changes take place more rapidly than non-material changes in social values, attitudes and social organisations. Extension education helps in bridging the gap created by the cultural lag by advising means of adjustment in the new environment. By this process the development of culture takes place.

Extension education uses information obtained and assembled from research studies all over the world, from experience wherever, it can be found and utilised and from the results of demonstrations performed for the purpose of extending knowledge. Rural people have different interests and needs and hence extension education has to be broad and varied in its meaning to meet the interests of the people it serves. It is an educational programme for the people, based on their needs and problems. It is designed to meet these needs and solve problems on a self-help basis. Thus, extension education is a teaching and learning process. It tries to bring out three types of changes in human behaviour.

a) Changes in knowledge or things known.
b) Changes in skills or things done.
c) Changes in attitudes or things felt.

In the first type of change an increased amount of useful information or understanding is provided to the people. It may be regarding the package of practices of wheat, methods of applying fertilisers or details about the marketing of agricultural products. In the second type of change new or improved skills, abilities and habits of the people are improved, such as how to avoid loss of vitamins while cooking the vegetables, how to harvest and transport vegetables for the market or spraying the correct type of insecticide for killing a particular crop pest. The third change is developing desirable attitudes and ideals in rural people, such as to make people believe that balanced diet is useful for human body, the importance of controlling soil erosion, or that yields can be increased by adopting improved farm practices. It will be clear from this that effective extension education contributes to the individual's understanding, helps him to improve his abilities and develops in him more desirable attitudes.

The concept of extension education is used in educating people about agriculture, industry, home science, dairy, veterinary science or public health. As per specialisation these branches of extension education are called agricultural extension, industrial extension, home science extension, dairy extension, veterinary science extension or public health extension.

Need

New inventions are giving rise to new technology. Farming is no exception to this phenomenon. The farmers need to be supplied with recent, useful and practical information related to agriculture. Agricultural development will be closely related with the development of the ability of the farmers' understanding and adoption of this technology. The researchers neither have the time nor are they equipped for the job of persuading the villagers to adopt scientific methods, and to ascertain from them the rural problems. Similarly it is difficult for all the farmers to visit the research stations and obtain firsthand information. Thus there is a need of an agency to interpret the findings of the research to the farmers and to carry the problems of the farmers to the research stations for solution. This gap is filled by the extension agency.

Importance

Extension uses democratic methods in educating the farmers. It respects the individuality of people in making their own decisions with the help of the extension worker. By this way the people grow in stature and self respect and are able to take rational decisions. Extension helps in the adoption of innovations. These innovations are of no use unless they are put to practical use. It is through extension that these new findings can reach the people speedily. Rural problems are numerous and are concerned with a large number of people spread over a large area. They can only be dealt with by an efficient extension agency meant for that purpose. The trained extension worker will understand the technology to be transferred among the farmers by studying their problems.

Scope

The scope of extension education includes all the activities directed towards the development of the rural people. The extension service must have dynamic programmes keeping pace with the constantly changing conditions. The following nine areas indicate the scope of extension work in rural areas.

1) Increasing efficiency in agricultural production.
2) Increasing efficiency in the marketing, distribution and utilisation of agricultural inputs and outputs.
3) Conservation, development and use of natural resources.
4) Proper mangement on the farm and in the home.
5) Better family living.
6) Youth development.
7) Leadership development.
8) Community development and rural development.
9) Improving public affairs for all-round development.

Philosophy

Philosophy is a body of general principles or laws of a field of knowledge. An individual, after considering pros and cons, decides on certain principles to guide his life. These principles play a vital role in deciding what is good or bad in the life of an individual. Goals and means are decided on the basis of these principles of life or the philosophy of life of an individual. For instance, the goal of two students studying in the same class may be to obtain good grades in the examination. However, they may adopt different approaches (means) for obtaining the grades in the examination based on their philosophies of life. One may work hard for obtaining the grades while another student may use unfair means for getting the grades. Two prisoners having different philosophies of life react differently to the same situation. Both of them look through the prison bars, one sees the mud and feels that the life is gloomy and becomes disappointed. Another prisoner looks at the sky and sees the stars and enjoys the atmosphere. It will be seen from these examples that the philosophy of life has relevance with the actions of the people. It provides a guide-line for performing the activities in life in a particular way.

The farmer is no exception to this principle. During the course of time he formulates a philosophy of life for himself. When an extension worker approaches him he tests the messages against his philosophy of life and if that message fits in his philosophy then he acts on it. If the extension worker approaches the farmers for the introduction of artificial insemination for their cows, a traditional minded farmer and a progressive farmer will react differently to his proposal. The progressive farmer may accept the proposal while the traditional minded farmer may reject the proposal.

Extension educational philosophy is based on the hypothesis that rural people are intelligent, are interested in obtaining new information and at the same time have a keen desire to utilise this information for their individual and social welfare. The krishi pandits and many progressive farmers are very intelligent. They obtain new information about scientific practices in farming and use it for increasing their yields. Certain organisations like gram panchayats, cooperatives, youth clubs, mahila mandals, etc., are created in the villages. These organisations undertake social welfare programmes for the community. The representatives of the people having different philosophies of life play a vital role in these welfare programmes.

The extension workers should utilise the latent goodwill of the people in extension programmes. A first step in this direction is to communicate new ideas and details of the welfare programmes to the people. An atmosphere of mutual trust and friendship between the extension workers and people should be developed. The extension worker should gain full understanding of the problems and difficulties of the people. This will help in solving the problems of the people. There are two ways of solving problems. One is by compelling people to act in a particular way by using coercive methods. Another way is by using a democratic approach, in which people are reached by educational methods to solve their problems.

In one hypothetical example Mosher explains the development due to compulsion and education.

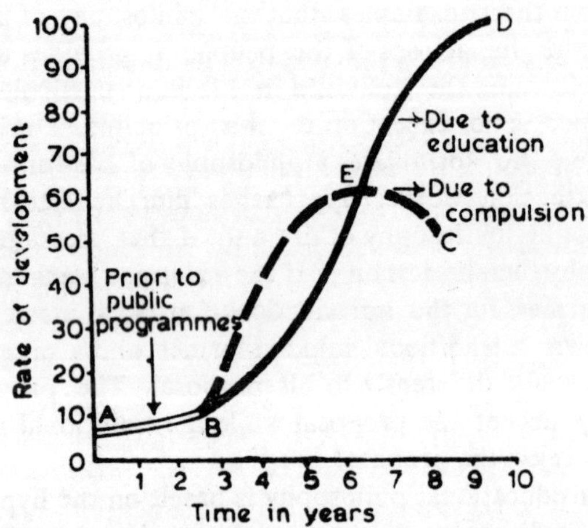

Fig. 1.1 Trend of Development Resulting from Programmes Using Compulsion and Those Using Educational Approaches.

In figure 1.1, AB is agricultural development before starting any public programme. BC is development by compelling the people to adopt certain improved farm practices, while BD is development due to education. It is seen that in the beginning the rate of agricultural development was more due to compulsion but it has fallen after point E. This means that in the beginning though the farmers accepted the practices under force, this change was not long lasting and they reverted back to their traditional practices in the long run. On the other hand, the rate of agricultural development due to education was slow in the beginning, but there was a rising trend after the intersection E. The farmers seem to have accepted the change by understanding its pros and cons. The change among them due to education was long lasting. Therefore, in the long run the educational programmes proved to be more effective than the compulsion programmes. It is therefore necessary that extension workers should have faith in the democratic values and should try to educate the people.

Extension work is developed on the principle of helping the rural people to stand on their feet. Economic development is given priority in the programmes of rural development. This would create strength in the people. By this strength they will develop their farms, homes, educational and recreational facilities which are necessary for their self-development and for national development. The rural people are to be helped in understanding their natural resources and the ways of utilising these resources for development. By utilising these natural resources they can lead a satisfactory life. Due to this reason the extension worker has to start from the level of the people and help them in utilising their resources for the betterment of individuals and the community.

The basic philosophy of extension is directed towards changing the outlook of man by educating him. As stated in the foregoing example, compulsion does not persuade the people to act in a particular way. The only way to secure the intelligent and wholehearted cooperation of a person is to educate him. Education is not a mere transfer of information. It is more than that. It's primary aim is to transform the people by bringing about desired changes in their knowledge, attitude and skills. If this has not happened then the activities chosen for extension are not educational and its effects cannot be long lasting.

Objectives

The objective of extension education is to raise the standard of living of the rural people by helping them in using their natural resources (like land; water and livestock) in the right way. Rural people are helped in planning and implementation of their family and village plans for increasing agricultural production, improving existing village crafts and industries. It should also help in providing minimum health, recreational, educational and housing facilities for improving family living conditions in the village. The specific objectives of extension education are given in the following lines.

1) Its fundamental objective is the development of the people.

2) To provide the farmers the knowledge and help that

will enable him to farm more efficiently and to increase his income.

3) To encourage the farmer to grow his own food, eat well and live well.

4) To promote better social, natural, recreational, intellectual and spiritual life among the people.

5) To help the members of the farm family to a larger appreciation of the opportunities, the beauty and the privileges of rural life and to know more about the world in which they live.

6) To open up new opportunities for rural people so that they may develop all their talents and leadership.

7) To build rural citizens who are proud of their occupation, independent in their thinking, constructive in their outlook, capable, efficient and self-reliant in character and have a love of home and country in their heart.

Principles

In the history of extension work, there are certain general principles of extension education which have been applied and tested. Some of these principles have more or less general application and therefore will be of use to the extension workers. With this view in mind they are presented in the following pages.

1) *Principle of Cultural Difference*

The educational methods should be in line with the culture of the people in order to make extension education effective. In a vast country like India different extension methods need to be used for different states, as people in these states differ in their thinking, living and culture.

There is a lot of difference in the culture and thinking of the people of U.P., Kerala and Tamil Nadu. Instead of using the same extension methods in all the states, it will be wise to study the history, culture, values, organisations and leadership of these areas and then make appropriate changes in the educational methods. Of course it is more difficult to recognise the attitudes, values, beliefs and traditions than to see the cultivation methods, use of improved implements, and farm size, etc. The extension worker has to recognise this difference between different cultures and use it in increasing the effectiveness of his work. The blueprint of the extension programme developed for one area may not be applicable as such in another area but it can serve as a guide in similar cultural areas. When the situation changes the old idea will have to be rejected and necessary alterations will have to be made in the programmes based on new ideas.

2) *Principle of Cultural Change*

The culture of people undergoes change while doing extension work. There will be change without extension work also, as change is necessary for the growth and development of society. To change the behaviour of the people through extension education, the extension worker should gain the confidence of the rural people. They should believe that what the extension worker says has relevance to their daily life. To start with, the extension worker should demonstrate the beneficial results of the useful ideas on the fields of some farmers so that they will have faith in him. Those who see the demonstration would tell others and all of them would realise that the extension worker has really something useful to contribute. They would discuss about their difficulties with the extension worker. The level of education of the people would rise from such simple events. First the extension worker has to help the farmer in increasing his yields, then he can concentrate on proper marketing of these increased yields. Taking the changes in the needs of the rural people into account the extension worker has to change his area of work. The situation prevailing twenty years ago when the extension service started and today is quite different and, therefore, with growth and development the extension work has to be changed to meet the cultural changes among the people.

3) *Principle of Grass-root Organisation*

Different groups work in rural communities. The extension worker should pay attention to the needs and interests of these groups while planning extension programmes. In some places the extension programmes are thrust on the people and the imposed innovations, many times have no relevance to the interests of these small groups. Unless the farmers feel that the ideas coming to them are useful they will not come ahead to adopt them. As the building based on sound foundation lasts long, similarly the programmes based on the needs and interests of these small groups would give better results in extension work.

4) *Principle of Cooperation*

The idea behind the extension work is the coming together of the rural people and the extension workers for social upliftment. The extension programmes should be the peoples' programme with government aid. All should cooperate and help each other for this task of social upliftment.

5) *Principle of Interests and Needs*

The rural people should voluntarily participate in the extension work. To be effective it should start from the interests and needs of the rural family. The extension education should fulfil these needs of the people and create interest among them for extension programmes. Many times the needs of the people and extension programmes are quite different. Sometimes the extension workers clearly see the important needs of the community but the people hold some other needs to be more important. In such cases the extension worker should give priority to the felt needs of the people. While doing this he should create an atmosphere of confidence, which would help in converting the unfelt needs of the people into the felt needs in future. The extension worker is also learning while giving the learning experience to the people. He starts from the experience and traditions of the people and leads them towards their development.

6) *Principle of Participation*

Many things are learned while doing a particular work. Good extension work helps the rural people in identifying their problems and then helping them in solving these problems. People will not feel attached to the work if they are given ready-made things. While constructing a school building or an approach road, if the people participate in kind or labour they develop a sense of belonging towards that project. This also develops leadership in the village and increases the confidence of the people. The extension worker can obtain the participation of the people by requesting the social leader to preside at a meeting. The extension worker in such instances can accept the role of an audience or secretary and help in fulfilling the objectives of the meeting. The leadership qualities are developed in rural people, if they participate in extension programmes. Confidently they come forward to undertake future programmes.

7) *Principle of Adaptability in the Use of Teaching Methods*

There are different people and groups in the village. These people differ in their level of understanding and knowledge and therefore, only one extension method will not be of use in providing information to all. Written material will be of use for those who can read it, radio programmes will be of use for those who listen to the radio, meetings will be of use for those who attend them and demonstrations will be of use to those who see them. Research shows that the use of more than one extension method carries the message effectively to the people. Due to the non-availability of communication facilities and at times due to carelessness, extension workers sometimes use only one extension method. It reduces the effectiveness of the message. At times, new methods must be devised to meet new situations and changing conditions.

8) *Principle of Leadership*

It is said that there is one leader in ten persons. Instead of working alone the extension worker should utilise this leadership for increasing the speed of extension work. After identifying these leaders they should be trained and encouraged to do extension work. Many people never know they had any ability in this direction until extension workers gave them the opportunity. Extension workers and specialists should train and orient these voluntary leaders for good extension work.

9) *Principle of Trained Specialists*

Like other sciences, agriculture, animal husbandry and the home sciences are moving forward rapidly. Therefore, maintaining competency in any one of these fields is a continuous job. In the constant effort of extension workers to keep abreast of changes, research and teaching personnel must help in many ways. If there are no trained specialists behind the extension work then extension cannot thrive. These specialists are the link between research and application of the research on farmers' fields. They have the responsibility of solving the problems of the extension workers in their subject. The subject matter specialist should have a broad outlook and he should know other subject matter fields related to family problems thereby concentrating on the welfare of the whole family and making his special contribution.

10) *Principle of Satisfaction*

The development programmes should lead to the satisfaction of the participants. The success of the extension work lies in the satisfaction of the people. If the people are not satisfied by participating in the programme, they will not participate in the future. Recognition and appreciation for work well done encourages voluntary leadership.

11) *Principle of the Whole Family Approach*

Extension work is for the whole family and it should reach all the members of the family. There should be place for the farmer, his wife and children in the programmes. Such programme will be useful and popular. While introducing innovations, if the extension worker neglects one member of the family there is a possibility of the rejection of the innovation. In U.P. a farmer sowed hybrid maize and increased his yields. But his wife did not like the *chapatti* prepared out of this maize as it had yellow colour. Yellow *chapatti* was considered as a sign of bad cooking in that community and, therefore, though the hybrid maize variety gave higher yields the family did not sow it the following year. Had the extension worker approached the housewife and come to know her views perhaps he could have avoided the rejection of the innovation.

12) *Principle of Evaluation*

It is necessary to determine the teaching results in an unbiased way. For this it is necessary to review the development made so far and see whether the extension work is proceeding in the right direction. If it is not, then it is necessary to take corrective measures. Extension work is educational in nature and therefore, its effectiveness should be measured by measuring the changes in people resulting from the teaching process. It is no longer enough to have only plans and methods but it is necessary to determine the teaching results by scientific ways. The results of such evaluations would help the extension workers in improving the quality of the programmes in the future.

13) *Principle of Applied Science and Democracy*

In democracy, freedom of thought and the unbiased and objective approach of the scientists, establish facts used in the solution of problems. Scientists, based on research, portray facts before the people but the people have the freedom to decide the adoption or rejection of the innovation. Extension has to carry the findings of the research to the rural people and show them its relation in fulfilling their needs. The results of research give a factual basis for the correction of common superstitions and unfounded beliefs that arose in the past from inaccurate observations. They are passed along from generation to generation in the folkways of the people. Applied agricultural science is not a one-way process. As it carries the findings of the research to the farmers it also takes back the problems of the people to the scientists for experimentation and for finding out necessary solutions.

Apart from the foregoing there are four principles on which the extension service rests. These principles are: (a) the citizen is the sovereign in the democracy, (b) the home is the fundamental unit of civilisation, (c) the family is the first training group of the human race, and (d) the average farm is endowed with great resources and facilities.

These are the principles of extension work. They are not universally applied in all the parts of the world due to differences in the types of farming, background and culture of people in different parts. However, they can be applied under new circumstances. In the first instance they may be tried experimentally and tested to see how well they work and how they can be properly changed to fit the conditions of the people.

EXTENSION EDUCATION SYSTEMS

Different extension educational systems or approaches were used in the past under the extension educational programmes. These systems can be grouped under four main headings; (1) the extension approach, (2) the training approach, (3) the cooperative self-help approach, and (4) the integrated development approach. These are not watertight, mutually exclusive compartments, nor are they purely educational classifications. They differ mainly, not in their educational principles and methods, but in their quite different underlying conceptions and theories of rural development. The details of each approach is given here.

1) Extension Approach

The extension approach uses the extension teaching methods for educating the people. It believes that the extension service can transform static economy into a dynamic economy. While improving the quality of family and community life, it emphasises the communication of information about innovative technical practices. It is mostly followed in America and Asia today and is referred to as the conventional or classical model of extension. This model was prepared by the professors of the land grant colleges who sought to make agricultural extension a separate scientific profession with its basic concepts, theory, principles and methodologies. The disciples who propagated this idea are the Americans and those who studied in the American universities. They helped to establish this model in many developing countries.

Objectives

The main objective is to persuade and help farmers in increasing agricultural production by adopting improved agricultural practices. It also aimed at improving the rural family life by educating the women and youth in the rural area.

Organisation

The extension service is mostly under the ministry of rural development or department of agriculture. It operates within the broad framework of national agricultural policies and objectives. It has a hierarchic structure with a network of trained field workers at the base supervised and guided by more highly qualified administrators and specialists at each of the three or more tiers (e.g. village, block, district, division, provincial and national levels). The extension service relies on the agricultural universities for the basic preparation of its personnel and for technical messages on research organisations of the ministry of agriculture and agricultural universities.

Educational Contents

The emphasis is on transfer of production technologies. It also helps in farm planning and management, use of credit, procurement of inputs and marketing of produce. The technical messages are relayed to local agents from the experts in the form of recommended practices for dissemination among the farmers.

The transfer of messages or information is done through extension methods for achieving rapid and widespread adoption of desirable innovations. This is done by achieving awareness, provoking interest, evaluation, trial by interested farmers on their own fields and adoption by convinced farmers. In some cases use of progressive leader farmers is made to produce the multiplier effect.

2) Training Approach

The training approach is considered to be related to the extension approach. But it has a different basic educational tradition and philosophy, closely related to institutionalised schooling. It emphasises more systematic and deeper learning of specific basic skills and related knowledge. Training programmes involve assembling learners in a training centre for a sustained period of instruction. These trained extension workers are supposed to transmit the useful knowledge gained by them to the rural people. It is based on the assumption that outsiders (extension workers) with superior knowledge and wisdom can help in solving the problems of rural society and lead them on the voyage of modernisation. The training and visit system is a good example of the training approach. This approach is based on the assumption that there is a gap between average productivity of various crops on the farmers' fields and the potential. This gap can be minimised by intensive extension efforts. The training and visit system evolved by Benor is being used in most of the developing countries with assistance from the World Bank to reduce this gap.

Objectives

The basic spirit behind the T & V system is that any land even though it may not have produced satisfactory crops in the past can be made to yield an optimum crop according to its capacity within the crop season. This can be done provided the farmer can be advised what to do on his own field, step by step according to the stage of crop growth. Thus the farmers are persuaded to adopt improved agricultural practices for increasing production.

Organisation

The extension service is mostly under the department of agriculture. The trained persons are posted at each level starting from the village to the national level. The training to the staff at the lower level is given by the subject matter specialists of the agricultural university and the department of agriculture. The messages or impact points for each crop are prepared in coordination with the agricultural university specialists and the staff of the departments of agriculture. These impact points are emphasised in the weekly and fortnightly training sessions. The staff then undertakes a visit programme for the transfer of know-how to the farmers.

Educational Contents

The emphasis is on training the staff of the department of agriculture and then transferring the know-how obtained at the training to the field staff. The technical messages are carefully selected and are relayed during visits to the farmers. The help of contact farmers is obtained in spreading these messages. The emphasis is more on giving on the spot guidance to the farmers in adopting new technology.

3) Cooperative Self-help Approach

The cooperative self-help approach starts with the assumption that the complex process of rural transformation must begin with changes in the rural people themselves. This change may be in their attitudes towards change, in their aspirations for improvement and in their perceptions of themselves. They should realise their own inherent power, individually and collectively, to better their conditions. The chief motive power for rural development must come from the people so that outside help of various kinds can be provided in response to the expressed needs of the people. There is heavy emphasis in this approach on the building of local institutions for cooperative self-help and governance. The example chosen for this approach is from Bangladesh. It is commonly known as the Comilla project as this approach was first used by the Academy of Rural Development at Comilla, in Bangladesh. The educational components of the Comilla project are of particular interest as they involved an extension service in which much of the efforts moved from bottom up instead of from top down.

Objectives

In this project the village people chose one of their own members to serve as their educational liaison with the outside services of knowledge relevant to their needs. This procedure was developed by the local cooperative societies and the Academy of Rural Development. Under this protocol the villagers agreed to: (1) organise themselves, choose a chairman and become a registered society, (2) hold weekly meetings, with compulsory attendance of all members, (3) select a man from the group and send him to the Academy once a week for training so that he could be the organiser and teacher of the group, (4) keep proper and complete records, (5) use supervised production credit, (6) adopt improved agricultural practices and skills, (7) make regular savings, (8) join the central cooperative association, and (9) hold regular member education sessions.

Organisation

The village cooperative thus became one of the prime agencies for agricultural education and rural education. The organiser becomes the key agricultural teacher in his own community, rather than the outside extension worker. Their representatives came regularly for training to the Academy and received expert advice and assistance on problems identified through discussions in the village cooperative society. The cooperatives became more organised and the operations became more complex. Afterwards the duties of an organiser and model farmer were combined in a cooperative manager who was paid on an incentive basis.

Educational Contents

Initially the training was restricted to the organiser but afterwards it provided skilled training in response to specific needs. For instance, school teachers and other literate villagers were trained to maintain the accounts of the village cooperatives. Young men were trained as tractor drivers and irrigation pump operators.

The Thana (district) Training and Development Centre emerged initially to meet the need for training local development, planning and coordination for new rural public works programme in the Comilla area. Due to the convenience of meeting the village teachers and cooperative manager, with one another and with representatives of the ministries and outside organisations, it became an important centre of development of the area. The educational processes were facilitated by the physical location of government officers with the Academy personnel and advisor at one place. It also facilitated the gradual acceptance by the official of a redefined role as teachers instead of desk-sitting issuers of directives and reports. Committees for training, extension and other functions, were made up of officials and advisors giving rise to established procedures and assignment of responsibility. As time passed the educational material supporting the process were refined to include simple extension lesson plans, booklets, manuals and other devices.

4) Integrated Development Approach

The integrated development approach emphasises the need of coordinating different agencies under a single management system of essential components (including education) required to get agricultural or rural development moving. The management system may be highly authoritarian, credit may be designed to provide an important role for local people in planning, decision-making and implementation of the programmes. The main emphasis is on rational development and coordination of all principal factors required for agricultural and rural development. The community development programme in India could not achieve the desired impact in increasing agricultural production. As a solution to this situation the intensive agriculture district programme (IADP) was launched in selected districts. The IADP used the integrated development approach in tackling the problem of rural development.

Objectives

In this programme there was more emphasis on the package approach. The ten points included in the programme were: (1) adequate farm credit through strengthened cooperatives; (2) adequate supplies of fertilisers, pesticides, improved seeds, implements and other essential production needs through strengthened service cooperatives; (3) price incentives to participating farmers through assured price agreements for rice, wheat and millet; (4) marketing arrangements and services to enable farmers to obtain a full market price for their marketed surplus; (5) intensive educational, technical and farm management assistance made available in every village; (6) participation of all interested farmers in farm planning for increased production; (7) village planning for increased production and village improvement programmes by strengthening village organisations and leadership; (8) a public works programme using local labour and development works contributing directly to increased production; (9) analysis and evaluation of the programme from its inception, and (10) coordination of all essential resources for maximum speed and effectiveness.

Organisation

Initially high potential districts were selected for IADP. Each district had a project director with a team of agricultural experts, working under the guidance and administrative control of the chief civil administrator. The team had the latitude to plan and implement the agricultural programmes fitted to the district and the resources available. These districts were accorded a special priority on fertilisers, credit and other essential supplies. Intensified research services, soil testing laboratories, and other similar facilities, were also provided to these IADP's.

Educational Contents

The staff under the community development programm was doubled in the IADP districts. Special agricultural information units were set up with their own printing presses and All India Radio's farm and home units were directed to give special attention to these districts. The multipurpose village level workers who were spending more time on other community programmes in addition to agriculture (e.g., health, nutrition, saving schemes, etc.) were now instructed to devote eighty per cent of their efforts to agriculture under the guidance of the block staff.

The bulk of the existing extension systems obviously do not coincide with one or other of these four systems. These four systems are in pure form and most of the systems combine elements of more than one approach. Nevertheless, the categories outlined provide a useful analytical structure for comparing the sample cases from the real world.

COMMUNITY DEVELOPMENT AND PANCHAYAT RAJ

After independence, it was imperative to change the outlook of the rural people living in villages. Their thinking and behaviour required to be moulded into patterns compatible with the modern age of science and technology. The constitution laid down that the state shall strive to promote the welfare of the people by securing and protecting as effectively as it may, a social order in which justice (social, economic and political), in national life will be provided.

Meaning

The community development programme was a step towards the realisation of that objective. It was defined as the process by which the efforts of the people are united with those of governmental authorities to improve the economic, social and cultural conditions of communities, to integrate these communities into the life of the nation and to enable them to contribute fully to national progress. In short, it is a process designed to create conditions of economic and social progress for the whole community with its active participation and the fullest possible reliance on community initiative. The important aspects of community development are advising the individual and the community to strive for self-improvement, making use of the available government assistance and obtaining people's participation.

Objectives

The objectives of community development are to help people to find the methods to organise self-help programmes and to furnish the techniques for cooperative action which the local people develop to improve their own culture.

The main objectives of the programme are:

a) Area development — with a minimum all round progress.

b) Self-help programme — people's participation being the essential feature.

c) Development of the whole community — with special emphasis on the weaker and underprivileged sections.

The aim of community development was to secure the fullest development of material and human resources in the area and thereby raise the rural community to higher levels of living. A rapid expansion in food and other agricultural production was prescribed as the primary objective of the programme since the shortage of food and raw materials was the greatest weakness of the country's economy. Allied to this objective, the development of cottage and small-scale industries for the purpose of providing employment to the non-agricultural classes who were not fully employed was also the purpose of community development. It was also realised that the problems of production and employment could not be solved satisfactorily without tackling the other needs of the villager. Emphasis was, therefore, laid on improvement of health and sanitation, provision of housing facilities and promotion of educational and other social activities. It was also recognised that lack of proper communication was a serious obstacle to the development of such facility. Provision of proper communication was also laid down as one of the objectives of this programme. Furthermore, considerable stress was placed on the importance of the training of agriculturists, artisans and extension workers of various kinds for proper implementation of the programme. But more important than all this, was the realisation that what was required was a change in the mental outlook of the people. The programme was to instill in them, an ambition for higher standards and the will to live a better life.

Evaluation of Panchayat Raj

Village panchayats have been in existence for long in India. With the advent of the British the panchayats were relegated to a subservient position in the colonial administrative set-up. Afterwards some efforts were made to revive them by forming local boards. A real push for the revitalisation of the panchayats was after independence when a certain specific role was assigned to them in administration. This was as per the constitution in which it is stated that the state shall take steps to organise village panchayats and to endow them with such powers and authority as may be necessary to enable them to function as units of self-government.

The first organised effort was through community development programmes in 1952. The programme emphasised the importance of working through people's institutions like village panchayats. It was to ensure their involvement in planning and implementation of development programmes and to secure the fullest possible public participation. In 1957 a study team was appointed by the Planning Commission to review the working of the community development programme and to examine the question of reorganising the district administration to provide for popular organisations between the village and state levels. This study team, headed by Balwantrai Mehta, recommended the setting up of elected bodies at village, block and district levels. Initially it was called the institution of democratic decentralisation and later on called as panchayat raj. The team suggested that these bodies should be entrusted with the task of planning and development. The basic principles emphasised in panchayat raj are:

a) It should be a three-tier structure of local self governing bodies from the village to district. These bodies should be organically linked up.

b) There should be a genuine transfer of power and responsibility to these bodies.

c) Adequate resources should be transferred to the new

bodies to enable them to discharge their responsibilities.

d) The system evolved should facilitate further devolution and dispersal of power and responsibilities in future.

The recommendations of the Mehta team gave a stimulus all over the country to an active consideration of decentralisation through democratic bodies. The Maharashtra government appointed a committee in 1961 under the chairmanship of Vasantrao Naik to examine the question of democratic decentralisation in Maharashtra. On the basis of the recommendations of the Naik committee the government enacted the Maharashtra Zilla Parishads and Panchayat Samiti Act 1961. In Maharashtra, village panchayats were already established under of the Bombay Village Panchayat Act 1958. The Maharashtra Zilla Parishads and Panchayat Samitis Act 1961, now provided for the establishment of zilla parishads at the district level and panchayat samitis in between the block level, supplying the necessary link between the village panchayats and zilla parishads.

Village Panchayat or Gram Panchayat is headed by a sarpanch. The sarpanch is elected by the members of the village panchayat. These members are elected by secret ballot from different wards. The functions of the village panchayats has already been discussed under the formal rural institutions. Panchayat samiti is the intermediate tier in panchayat raj. It is headed by a chairman who is elected by ballot by the panchayat samitis from amongst its members. The members of the panchayat samiti are the councillors of the zilla parishad elected from the electoral division included in the block and the sarpanch of the village panchayats is elected by members of panchayats in accordance with the provisions of the act. The panchayat samitis are entrusted with development functions and are directly responsible for the implementation of the community development programme. They are also charged with the preparation and implementation of developmental plans for the block. The samiti is vested with specific executive responsibilities in the matter of primary education, health, sanitation and communication. They also supervise the work of village panchayats and have the right to scrutinise the budget of panchayats. Zilla parishad is at the district level and is headed by president. He is elected by the parishad from amongst its elected councillors by ballot. The members of the zilla parishad consist of representatives of the panchayat samitis, members directly chosen by the people by direct election from electoral divisions in the district and coopted members. The zilla parishad exercises general supervision over the working of the panchayat samitis and advises the government on the implementation of the development schemes. Besides these duties, it has specific executive functions in the establishment, maintenance and expansion of secondary, vocational and industrial schools.

The panchayat samitis and zilla parishads function through standing committees set up to look after specific items of work like education, planning, industries, social welfare, finance, etc.

MISCONCEPTIONS ABOUT EXTENSION

There are several misconceptions about the nature of extension and its outcome. Sometimes it is misunderstood that extension work can be attached to already existing jobs like research, teaching or regulatory jobs. These jobs are different than the extension job and if they are asked to carryout the extension work then their original work is bound to suffer. Sometimes their original work and additional extension work may create role conflict. This may result in creating a confused image of the workers in the minds of the people which may hinder their role performance. Extension is a fulflezed work and it need to be considered in that light by establishing a separate extension organization. This organization has to reach large number of people, maintain contacts with subject matter and other related input agencies.

For many people, Science means physics, Chemistry and such other physical sciences only. However, besides physical sciences there are biological sciences like, botany, zoology etc and social sciences like economics, sociology, psychology etc. Extension Education is basically a applied social science. It is a science of making people innovative. The people are free to reject or adopt the information provided by the extension agency as extension is educational in nature. The extension worker used persuasive approach, for which he should know the technology and the local situation. Thus the extension worker has to be an area specialist i.e. he should know the details of environment in which the new information can be fitted. Extension is criticised because it is sometimes in-effective. in persuading people to adopt a particular recommendation. Most of this technology originates outside the extension organization and therefore special linkages for providing this information need to be established. Many a times this information is inaccurate and biased which questions the credibility of the extension organization. The technology being promoted may not be appropriate or poorly suited to conditions of farmers. The other reasons for ineffectiveness may be inadequate resources, poorly trained field staff, mobility problems, few teaching resources and in some cases the field staff is assigned with too many non extension responsibilities that can result in role conflict.

CHAPTER 2

Extension Educational Psychology

Educational psychology is the systematic study of the development of the individual within the educational setting. Human behaviour can be understood, predicted and directed towards desired goals by applying the principles of educational psychology. From the time he is born until his death an individual continues to learn new things. Educational psychology studies the individual through the life stages as he acquires new knowledge.

Educational psychology is one of the branches of applied psychology concerned with the application of the principles, techniques and other resources of psychology to the solution of the problems confronting the teacher. It is helpful to the teacher whose aim is to direct the growth of students towards defined objectives. The objectives of education are not decided by educational psychology. They are normally decided by normative sciences such as ethics and philosophy. But once it is decided, educational psychology will help in attaining it. As stated earlier, educational psychology is concerned with the educative process from birth to death of an individual. Thus, the scope of educational psychology is concerned with this educational process which includes the following areas of the learner: developmental characteristics, individual differences, intelligence, personality and mental health of the learner. The learning process includes the psychology of learning, motivation of learning, factors affecting learning and diagnosis of learning problems. Lastly, the scope includes the evaluation of the learning performance by conducting research in education.

Basic Concepts

Instincts

Instincts are complex inherited tendencies common to all members of a species compelling each individual, (i) to perceive and pay attention to certain objects and situations; (ii) to experience positive or negative emotional excitement on perceiving them; and (iii) thereupon to act in a way which is likely in the long run to preserve the individual. Some of the common instincts are parental, gregariousness, sex, self-assertion, escape, acquisition, etc. These instincts are observable in people and animals. A child is playing with toys. Suddenly there is noise of thunder and a flash of lightening outside. The child leaves the toys and runs weeping to his mother. The child moved away due to the instinct of escape. He ran to his mother for protection.

Drive

The term need is closely related with drive. Need refers to a condition of lack or deficiency in the organism. The need for food for maintaining the physiological state of hunger drives the individual in search of food. Hence, need for food gives rise to the hunger drive. Drive is defined as a tendency initiated by shifts in the physiological balance in the body. The individual is restless because of drive. Thus drives are the sources of energy.

There is drive reduction or need satisfaction when an individual gets food. A child becomes restless when he is hungry. The hunger drive increases tension in him. When the child is fed by the mother, there is reduction in the drive as the need is satisfied. Drive reduction is now associated with the mother and milk. On similar occasions, the child will try to satisfy the need through his mother. Thus the behaviour of the child gets a direction. This goal-directed behaviour is called motivation.

Motive

Motive is that which moves or activates. In psychology it refers to some internal activator within an individual. The motives are the directing tendencies inside the individual to follow a particular course of action. A puppet moves when its strings are manipulated. Its movements are forced upon it. The puppet is without motivation as the movement cannot be attributed to any motive of the puppet. But motives are goal directed.

Motivation is energy mobilisation towards the attainment of goals. The motive joins a state of energy mobilisation and a goal. Without motivation the energy will be diffused through aimless activities. The motivation will depend on the needs of the learners. The order of needs of human beings from lower (basic) to higher levels include physiological needs, e.g., hunger; safety needs, e.g., security; sense of belonging needs, e.g., affection; esteem needs, e.g., prestige; and need for self-actualisation, e.g , desire for self-fulfilment. The basic needs are more dominant in the first instance in the life of an individual. Once they are satisfied he tries to seek satisfaction of the higher order needs. The teacher should identify the needs of the learners and motivate them towards fulfilling these needs. The students will not be interested in learning if there is no proper motivation.

Attitude

Attitude is the degree of positive or negative feelings associated with some psychological object towards which people differ in varying degrees. It is developed in three phases, firstly towards the object, then the effect connected with the object, and finally the action that can be undertaken with respect to that object. Attitudes are not innate but are formed as a result of the individuals contact with the object and its environment.

The attitude affects an individual's course of action. Due to unfavourable attitudes towards the family planning programme an individual is not likely to participate and follow the recommendations of the programme. In such a situation the first job of the change agent is to make efforts for changing the attitude of the person. The change in attitude may lead to action.

Intelligence

Individuals differ in their ability to learn, to adjust to new situations, manage things, persons and ideas. This difference is due to the intelligence level of the individuals. Intelligence is defined as the capacity of solving problems by using past experience, adjusting with new things and understanding abstract things by using symbols. Binet evolved intelligence tests to discriminate intelligent students from lazy ones. He made sets of questions for children of different age groups. By asking questions to each age group he evolved a concept of mental age (M.A.) which is indicative of the intellectual development of the individual. This mental age was related with chronological age (C.A.) to obtain the intelligence quotient (I.Q.) of the individual.

$$\text{Intelligence quotient} = \frac{\text{Mental age}}{\text{Chronological age}} \times 100$$

OR

$$\text{I.Q.} = \frac{\text{M.A.}}{\text{C.A.}} \times 100$$

If a child of 8 can do all the tests meant for the 10 year-olds, then his M.A. = 10 and his I.Q. $= \frac{10}{8} \times 100 = 125$. If he can only do the tests for 6 year-olds then his mental age is 6 and his I.Q. $= \frac{6}{8} \times 100 = 74$. However, if he can perform successfully on all the tests meant for children aged 6 and also some of the tests intended for 7 and 8 year-olds, his score of M.A. will be more than 6 depending on the proportion of the tests for the higher age groups that he is able to perform correctly.

The individuals in any community range from idiots to a very brilliant level of intelligence. The extension teaching should start from the level of the farmers. The farmers of different intellectual capacities will be frustrated if they are tought by only one method and similar material. The intelligent farmer will be bored and the feeble minded will not be able to understand. It will be better if the farmers are categorised on the basis of their intellectual level and lessons are planned according to their capacities.

Culture

Culture is defined as the socially standardised ways of feeling, thinking and acting which an individual acquires as a member of the society. Man is not born with culture. He learns it through parents, friends, and social institutions. Culture is shared by the members of the society. Each individual plays his role in satisfying the needs and interests of the society. Culture provides specific ways of satisfying the physical and social needs of the individual. Culture defines situations, goals, attitudes, values and behaviour patterns. Culture, therefore, reduces or restricts the range of alternative means available to the individual. In the Indian situation, most of the rural communities are tradition bound. The farmer has usually no choice other than accepting the narrowly defined means approved by the culture. Thus culture influences, controls and directs the behaviour of an individual in society.

Socialisation

Socialisation is the process of inducting the individual into the social and cultural world to play his role as a member of society. In socialisation the inherited potential of the persons is developed under proper conditions. The process of socialisation starts from the birth of an individual. He comes in contact with the family members who teach him many things. A child reared in a friendly atmosphere will develop a different type of personality as compared to another child reared in a hostile atmosphere. Then an individual comes in contact with school. He keeps the ideal of the parents at home and the teacher in school. His circle of friends also plays a vital role in his socialisation. The man is known by the company he keeps. Other social contacts also affect the process of socialisation. The personality of an individual emerges out of this process of socialisation.

Personality

Personality is the dynamic organisation within the individual of those psychological systems that determine the unique adjustments to his environment. Personality is not static but a dynamic concept which is continuously changing and growing. A child, when he grows up develops a different type of personality. Personality is not something with which an individual starts his life but it is what he acquires and develops in the course of life and experience. It includes the psychological systems in him. It is the integrated unity of all aspects of his being, i.e., his physical, social and mental faculties. Personality is distinctive or unique in its adjustment to the environment. Two persons will react differently to the same environment due to their personalities.

Several attempts are made to classify personalities. Classifications of personality are based on emotional trends, physical and psychological structure and social relationships. In an universal categorisation Jung classified personalities as introvert and extrovert. An introvert is more interested in evaluating himself, better at writing than at speaking, inclined to worry, easily embarrassed, fond of reading, reserved, likes to be alone, lacks flexibility and is careful of his personal belongings. An extrovert is social, adaptable, interested in people, fluent in speech, free from worries, not easily embarrassed, likes to work with others and wants to be in the limelight. Most of the people are not extreme introverts or extroverts in traits but fall somewhere between the two extremes. Such people are grouped as ambiverts.

The objectives of extension education are educational in nature. The effort of the change agent is to change the knowledge, skill and attitudes of the farmers so that their personality undergoes change. This changed 'man' is expected to make use of modern advances in science for solving the problems surrounding him.

Teaching

As stated in the communication model the communicator or teacher has to initiate the message and pass it on to the intended audience. In other words, he has to do the job of a teacher. Teaching is the process of arranging situations that stimulate and guide the learning activity towards the goals that specify desired changes in the behaviour of the learners (effect). It consists of providing situations in which the important things to be learned are called to the attention of the learners, their interest developed, desire aroused and action promoted.

Factors Contributing to Teaching

Successful teaching contributes to effective learning. The factors contributing to good teaching are discussed here.

1) Teaching based on the needs of people: Teaching should be related to the life situations and problems of the learners. How the learning will help in solving the need of the learner should be explained to him.

2) Natural impulse of the learners should be used in training: All development and education start with basic needs and drives. The teaching material should be organised in an interesting way so that the learners take interest in learning.

3) Appropriate aids should be used along with new presentation: A visual appeal is the most effective approach. A picture or model presented for a short period will produce a more vivid image than a verbal description.

4) Physical conditions should be satisfactory: Physical comforts, proper ventilation, lighting, etc., eliminate discomfort and help in learning.

5) The course should be organised from the standpoint of learners: The learners should know what the subject matter is and how it is going to benefit them.

6) The teacher should develop a pleasing personality: The teacher should try to develop in himself patience, helpfulness, clarity, firmness, a sense of humour, cheerfulness, sincerity and sympathy.

7) The teaching should be intimately tied to its practical application: If the learner is given an opportunity to try out the things learned then it develops his understanding. Good teaching helps in problem solving and making a clear impression on the minds of the learners.

Steps in Extension Teaching

In order to bring about the desired changes in the behaviour of people the teacher needs to organise activities so that there will be repetition of the desired behaviour. This deliberate organisation of teaching activities in a sequence greatly increases the efficiency of learning. The teacher plans and arranges situations and activities whereby the thing to be learned is called to the attention of the prospective learner, his interest developed, desire aroused and action promoted. In effective teaching there are six steps (figure. 2.1).

1) Attention: Farmers are not always aware of the improvements they can make as the result of scientific research and

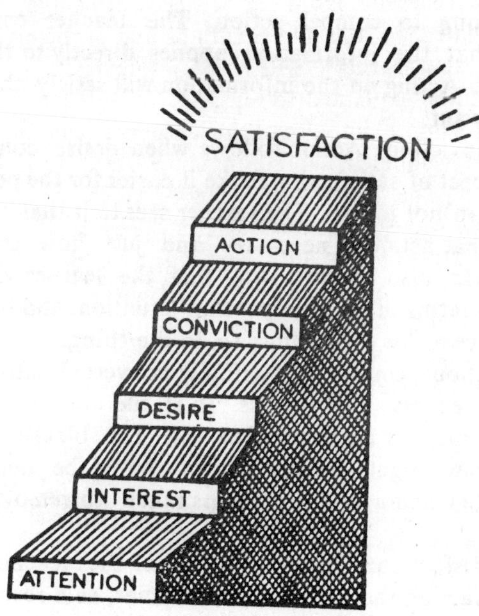

Fig. 2.1 Steps in Extension Teaching.

successful experience of other farmers. In such instances the first task of the extension teacher is to direct the attention of the prospective learner to, the new or better idea. Until the individual's attention has been focussed on the change that is considered desirable, there is no recognition of a problem to be solved or a want to be satisfied. Attention is the starting point to the arousing of interest.

2) Interest: Once attention has been captured it becomes possible for the teacher to appeal to the basic needs or urges of the individual and arouse his interest in a further consideration of the idea. The teacher reveals to the learners that the new skill or practice will contribute to the learners welfare. The teacher should present the message attractively and in a manner that requires little mental effort on the part of the learner. The presenting of one idea at a time, which is definite and specific, is an important factor in building interest.

3) Desire: The teacher is concerned with the continued stimulation of the learner's interest in the new idea or practice

until that interest becomes a desire or motivating force sufficiently strong to compel action. The teacher convinces the learner that the information applies directly to the learner's situation. Acting on the information will satisfy the learner's need or want.

4) Conviction: Action follows when desire, conviction and the prospect of satisfaction make it easier for the person to act rather than not to act. The teacher sees to it that the learner knows what action is necessary and just how to take that action. He also makes sure that the learner visualises the action in terms of his own peculiar situation, and has acquired confidence in his own ability to do the thing.

5) Action: Un less conviction is converted into action the teaching efforts are useless. It is the job of the teacher to make it easy for the learner to act. The blocks and annoyances that might prevent action should be anticipated by the teacher and appropriate steps taken to remove or bypass them.

6) Satisfaction: The end product of the teaching effort is the satisfaction that comes to the learner, as a result of solving a problem, meeting a need, acquiring a new skill or some other change in behaviour. Follow up by the teacher helps the learner to evaluate the progress made, strengthens the satisfactions, minimises the annoyances and builds the learner's confidence in his ability to continue action with increasing siatisfaction. The goals of learning should be kept simple and within the ability of the learner so that he can derive satisfacton of its achievement. The satisfaction and confidence resulting from the successful completion of each small job will then lead logically to the accomplishment of the difficult jobs, 'A satisfied customer is the best advertisement' applies to extension worker as well as to the retail merchant.

The extension teacher has to arrange the learning situations in all the six teaching steps with the help of the extension teaching methods. Various teaching methods are not equally suited to advance each of the different steps in teaching, each method under certain circumstances makes a contribution to each step. It depends on the teacher how he handles the situation.

Learning

The receiver is the intended audience of the messages. The receivers learn through seeing, hearing about and doing the thing to be learned. Learning is the process by which a person changes his behaviour through his own efforts.

Principles of Learning

In extension education the main emphasis is on providing effective learning experiences to the rural people. While doing so the extension worker or the communicator should know the characteristics of learning. These are also called principles of learning.

1) Learning is growthlike and continuous: The extension worker should understand the level of the farmer and should try to develop his understanding. The relationship between the things the farmer knows and the new ideas should be clarified with the help of education. The subject should be presented in such a way that the farmers should understand it. The new ideas may be repeated intermittently to emphasise its importance.

2) Learning should be meaningful: The farmer will understand the value of things learned or taught to him only when he can see its utility in practical life. If immediate opportunity to use the knowledge obtained through learning is available then the knowledge is retained for a longer time. The extension worker should therefore place the objectives of learning very clearly and meaningfully before the farmers. While doing this, care has to be taken to see that the subject does not go over the heads of the farmers. This is especially important in extension education as the educational programme needs to be situation oriented and within the physical and economic limits of the people. While administering the extension programmes what changes are expected in the clientele should be clearly known to the change agent. The clear objectives will serve as a guide in undertaking the programmes and also at the time of evaluation.

3) In learning maximum senses of the learners should be used: Senses are the gateways to mind. Seeing, hearing, touching, smelling and tasting are the five senses through which an individual learns new ideas. In extension mostly the messages

are received by the people by seeing, hearing and doing new things. Some people learn by hearing while some believe on what they see. For making the teaching effective the learner's maximum senses should be utilised. The capacity of learning is mainly dependent on the use of the senses and creative thinking on the part of the learner. One aspect of effective teaching is to present a constructive and desirable picture of the result before the eyes of the learners. Demonstrations, visual aids and other symbols help in making this picture of a new idea more vivid in order to make the learning experiences effective.

4) Learning should be challenging and satisfying: The motivation to learn comes out of the interest of the learner but the learning becomes useful and effective if the teacher arranges good learning situations. The farmers should be encouraged for timely and proper progress. Of course care must be taken to see that the expected educational level should be within the capacity of the farmers. The extension worker should place a challenging picture of new things before the farmer and convince him that he can have satisfaction by learning new things. While doing this a friendly atmosphere should be maintained.

5) Learning should develop functional understanding of learners: It is not enough for the extension worker to provide knowledge in teaching, but the knowledge imparted should be understood by the farmers. After understanding the new ideas the farmer should be able to utilise them in real life situations. Acquiring knowledge is the first step in learning and it is different from understanding. Memorising is one way of acquiring knowledge but unless this knowledge is used in everyday life it will be forgotten. Unless the farmer puts into use what he learned, his learning is of no use in reaching the desired objectives. To develop the functional understanding of the farmer it is necessary that he should understand the whole subject as well as different topics and their interrelationships. If a farmer is interested in using fertilisers for his wheat crop then he should understand the dose, time and method of application as well as the interrelationship between these elements so that he can use the fertiliser judiciously.

In learning why a particular thing is to be learned it

utility in life should be emphasised in the beginning. After understanding the need of new information it may be divided into parts. The function of each part, its relation with other parts and finally the relation of each part to the whole topic should be clearly understood. Then the farmer would decide the place of the new idea in his work and utilise the new information in his everyday life. The extension worker should divide the extension programmes in meaningful parts and decide the methods to be used in making the learning effective.

6) Learning is affected by physical and social environment: The physical and social environment creates a favourable background for effective learning. The physical environment includes temperature, light, aeration and sitting arrangements. The student should be required to spend minimum energy in adjusting with the environment. Social environment and the mental make up of the student are closely associated. The teacher should create a suitable environment.

7) Learning ability varies widely among individuals: There needs to be a balance between the level of understanding of the farmers and the level of communication. Similarly the subject should be within the capacity of the farmers' ability to learn. Extension programmes should be organised by taking this individual variation into account.

8) Learning, in general, is a gradual process, usually requiring several exposures before change is noticed: In extension education it is expected that the rural people should use improved practices in their fields, homes and villages. The main emphasis is on doing things by the rural people for all-round development of the village. Education should result in action by the people. The new ideas have to be vividly presented through different media in order to make the learning fruitful. If the extension worker intends to introduce an innovation then he should tell about it to the local leaders and progressive farmers. This contact will be of use to him while conducting meetings and informing other people. Depending on the nature of the innovation, demonstrations and distribution of particular materials will have to be undertaken. If the extension worker can create a picture of what is to be learned, why it is to be learned and to what extent it is to be learned then the people will

voluntarily come ahead to learn new things. Research shows that for convincing the necessity of innovation it has to be presented at least six to eight times through different media.

9) The adults have learning capacity: All adult education programmes are based on the assumption that the adults have the capacity to learn new things. Learning capacity, starting about the age of six increases rapidly until age 20, then it begins to level off until around 50. The rate of learning declines about one per cent a year after the age of 35. The main reason for this declining capacity among the adults is their eyesight, hearing capacity and low external motivations. In addition to this there is reluctance to learning, because of fear of failure, old habits and impact of a particular ideology.

The extension worker should arrange the use of equipment so that all can see clearly. The adults comprehend spoken words with less difficulty and therefore the extension worker should speak clearly by choosing words carefully. Proceed step by step and repeat the ideas which you are trying to get across. Encourage good ideas and reward progress. It is necessary to avoid ridicule and punishment.

10) Learning is an active process on the part of the learner: The extension worker can create an atmosphere for learning but the farmer will have to learn by himself. For learning new skills the farmer must practise them. He must relate the facts in order to understand them. For creating new attitudes he must change the present attitudes. Similarly he has to develop appreciation for new things. All people do not learn at the same time and at the same rate but if they are taught together then the learning becomes easier for them. The farmer in such a situation not only learns from the extension worker but also by discussion with his colleagues.

11) Learning requires effective communication: In communication, new ideas are carried to the people. In this process two or more individuals communicate their feelings, ideas, thoughts and opinions. They share similar experiences. Communication is necessary for effective extension education. In communication, mostly words are used but it can be more effective if visuals and symbols are shown to the people. The symbols used in communication should be appropriate to the

situation in order to clarify ideas.

12) Theory and practice should be related in learning. Theory explains the why and how of an idea. Sometimes though a student understands theory he cannot use it in practice. On the other hand in some instances the student knows how to do a particular thing but does not know the theory behind it. There should be a balance between the two and for acquiring high professional competency it is necessary to know both theory and practice. As far as possible the farmers should be taught both.

Learning Situation

Extension teaching is a process of creating situations that are conducive to effective learning, and learning is a process through which changes in behaviour are achieved. So the job of the extension worker is to arrange proper learning situations in which the farmer will be able to learn. As already emphasised, learning takes place through learning experiences. In extension education, the learning of the rural people will be effective if a proper learning situation is arranged and effective learning experiences are provided. This will help in achieving the objectives of extension education. A good extension worker should have faith in people, he should possess technical knowledge and the ability to use this knowledge with foresight in solving the problems of people. He should emphasise on creating basic changes in the people rather than trying to fulfil their immediate needs. He should provide technical knowledge to the people through extension methods by bringing them together. He should also help them in converting that knowledge into practice.

Learning is an active and intentional process on the part of the farmer. It takes place through experiences and therefore, the extension worker should organise effective learning situations in which the rural people can have good learning experiences. These experiences may be through mental or physical action.

The good learning situation has the following five elements:

1) A skilful extension worker.
2) Farmers who want and need to learn.
3) Subject in line with the needs and abilities of the learners

or farmers.

4) Teaching equipment and materials adequate for the farmers.

5) Satisfactory physical arrangements.

The extension worker should skilfully manipulate the elements of the learning situation and provide satisfactory learning experiences to the people. As pointed out in figure 2.2,

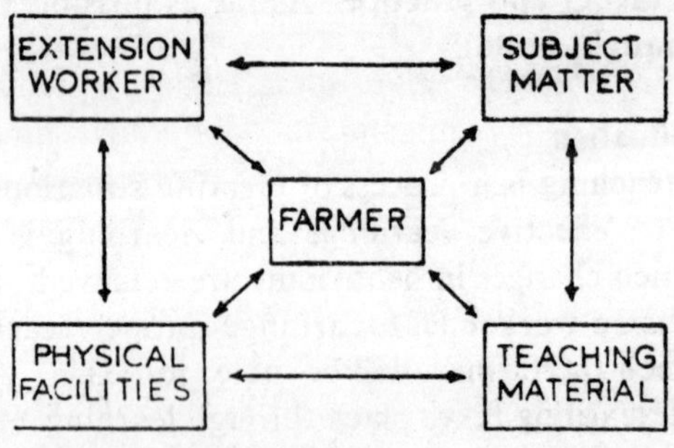

Fig. 2.2 The Learning Situation.

the farmer is a centre of the learning situation and the other four elements act on it. The main aim of extension education is to alter the behaviour of the farmers and the other elements are supported to help this process. The success of the learning situation should be judged from the desirable atmosphere it has created for effective learning.

In order to be effective the extension worker must speak clearly so that the farmers can understand him. He must know the level of the farmers in terms of their knowledge of subject matter, level of education, interest in the subject matter, need for the subject matter, and opportunities to apply what is learned. He must be clear about the objectives of teaching and present a vivid picture of the objectives to the farmers. He must be skilful in using the extension methods in order to communicate the messages effectively. Every lesson should be planned properly. Many times the farmers are distracted by the habits of the extension worker. If the extension worker has a habit of repeating the words 'Do you understand?'

then the farmers may pay attention to this habit more than the subject being taught.

The farmers should have interest in the subject matter. They should have the need, the ability to understand and the opportunity to apply the subject matter. They should have mental and physical preparation for learning. After learning they should be clear in their mind regarding the use of the subject matter.

The subject matter should be in line with the needs and interests of the farmers. It should be properly organised with valid, authentic, factual and applicable information. It should be at a level where it can be understood by the farmers.

The teaching equipment and materials should be readily available and should be suitable for the subject matter. They should be in working condition so that they can be operated properly.

The physical facilities like light, ventilation, sitting arrangement or the outdoor facilities should be as satisfying and comfortable as possible. All these arrangements should be made before starting the class or meeting.

Apart from the aforementioned elements, individual points of view, individual difficulties, the opinion of the community about that topic, outside noises and the like, affect learning. The extension worker should try to reduce the bad effects on learning and help in creating a favourable situation so that the farmers can devote more time and energy in learning. In short the situation should be such in which the farmer should be in a position to learn with full concentration. The extension worker, by studying the problems can create a favourable environment in which the rural people can learn effectively. By doing this he would help in achieving the objectives of extension education effectively.

Learning Experiences

The job of the extension worker is to direct the learning process by which the farmer, through his own activity, becomes changed in behaviour. As pointed out by Hammonds, good extension teaching is directing the activities of the farmer so as to result in the larger amount of the most desirable intended learning and the smallest amount of undesirable learning.

By and large, good extension teaching brings about effective learning by providing effective learning experiences to the rural people. The ultimate criterion for success in extension teaching are the results in terms of change in the rural people. This means how far the teaching lasts and how far the farmer can and does use it in his life. Badenhop clarified this role when he said that the results of teaching that a farmer can and does use freely, flexibly, and confidently in his life are clearly far superior to those which he can produce only when he is given the right clue or asked the right question. A young farmer, while running a tractor in the field, accidentally dropped a steel nut into the engine of the tractor. Instead of having the tractor towed to the garage, he attached a wire to the battery and wrapped it around a steel rod, thus making an electromagnet with which he easily recovered the nut. He gave credit, of this ingenious plan to his science teacher in high school, who he said had 'taught him to think'. Teaching should be such that the learners could use the results freely and flexibly in their lives.

It will be clear from the foregoing discussion that the information of providing learning experiences to the learner should be known to all who are engaged in educational affairs. It should not be locked with the theorists and specialists in this field. The farmer learns new ideas by mentally and physically undergoing the learning experiences. In these learning experiences the farmer knows and understands new ideas by critical observation, hearing and by doing. This knowledge and understanding helps the farmer in solving the problems in his future life.

The extension worker should, therefore, arrange a learning situation in which the farmer will have effective learning experiences. But the extension worker cannot shirk his responsibility by only creating a learning situation, he has to see that the behaviour of the farmer is directed to effective learning experience. A large amount of learning will depend on what exactly the farmer or extension worker does in that situation. The syllabus and curriculum are important and provide a guideline to both learner and the teacher. Reading a book, attending a training class, hearing a lecture or observing the extension programme are some of the activities in which there is the idea of providing learning experiences. These activities though important are not sufficient for learning experiences. In a similar learning situation the experiences of two students can be different. In one meeting the extension specialist provided an information to the village level workers. Both the village level workers were provided with equal opportunity for learning the new information, but there was difference in their learning. The first village level worker heard the information with keen interest and by deep thinking tried to understand the interrelationship among different elements. Then he related this knowledge to his previous experience. Afterwards he applied this increased knowledge in solving the problems and difficulties of the people of his area. Wherever he failed to understand the new information he again approached the specialist and got them explained. Thus by creative thinking this village level worker understood the information and used it for the benefit of the people of his area. In short, this village level worker has undergone effective learning experiences. The reaction of the second village level worker was the exact opposite. He had no interest in the information of the specialist. His mind was preoccupied with some other topic while hearing the lecture of the specialist and therefore he heard the lecture intermittently. Due to this he could not understand the information completely with the result he could not have the main theme of the information provided by the specialist. In short, this village level worker did not learn anything and could not apply it for the benefit of the people of his area.

In order to bring the desired objectives of the programme into reality it is important to provide effective learning experiences to the clientele. It is necessary to decide beforehand the learning experiences to be provided to the learners. This would change their behaviour and they would move in the desirable direction.

Many methods of providing effective learning experiences are available to the extension worker. These methods are not only opinions but are based on research and experience. The extension workers should know them thoroughly before organising them into learning experiences for the rural people.

1) The farmers should be provided a chance of undergoing learning experience in the direction of the desired change. If

the objectives include mental or physical skill then the farmers should be given an opportunity to learn that skill since that is the only way through which they can internalise it. A specialist teaching a student of blacksmithy the selection of an iron piece, its heating to a particular temperature and then the using of the hammer to convert that iron piece into a shear of iron plough needs to provide an opportunity for the learner to do these things for himself. Without doing this for himself he cannot be a good blacksmith. Once the learner knows the thing to be done he can acquire the skill by constant efforts. If it is desired that the farmer should learn mental skill in solving problems, then he should be provided opportunities for solving such problems.

2) After undergoing the learning experience, as per the objectives of teaching the farmer should feel satisfied. For showing the problems of a balanced diet in a family it will not be enough to teach the farmers the method of better cooking of vegetables but care will have to be taken to see that the members of the family feel satisfaction in eating the cooked vegetables. If the cooked vegetable is distasteful or the learning experience unsavoury to them then they will discontinue that practice, and learning will not take place.

3) The learning experiences should be within the mental and physical capacity of the farmers. This means that the extension worker should start from the level of the farmers. The farmers should be given the opportunity and time for action. Necessary finance and material needs to be made available. If the practical aspect in the learning experience situation is beyond the capacity of the farmer then naturally the aim of teaching will not be achieved. To avoid these pitfalls the extension worker should know the economic, social and physical surroundings of the farmers properly.

4) The extension worker should provide proper learning experiences which would lead to desirable objectives. The objectives of education as emphasised earlier can only be achieved through these learning experiences. This is an important part in education, and as per the situation the extension worker should provide different learning experiences. Learning does not take place automatically, it has to be based on some basic principles and effective operational methods.

5) One learning experience usually helps in achieving more than one objective and this reality helps in achieving the long term objectives of extension education. An individual trying to solve the agricultural problems of the rural people will collect more information due to curiosity about agriculture and while doing this he will also learn many things.

6) The extension worker should be capable of providing the learning experiences. If he does not know the method he has to teach or does not know the operation of the implement which he wants his students to operate then he cannot provide those learning experiences to his students. It affects their learning to a great extent.

It will be clear from the foregoing discussion that the selection and use of learning experiences is not a mechanical process. It requires creative thinking on the part of the xtension worker. He has to be careful in selecting the learning experiences which would lead towards the achievement of the desired objectives. For this purpose he should prepare a lot of such helpful learning experiences. While doing this he should see that the type of information and education facilities needed (e.g., books, slides or posters, etc.) are available with him. This list can be long but keeping the objectives in sight these methods should be carefully chosen. Secondly, the learning experiences which the extension worker intends to provide should be given a serious thought. It would include the action to be taken by the farmer, his reading of a book or reading a part of the book or discussion, the experiences of other farmers in solving similar problems, etc. The list can be long but without diverting from the objectives of extension education the learning experiences should be carefully chosen and provided to the rural people.

EXTENSION EDUCATIONAL PSYCHOLOGY

It is seen that learning and psychology are closely related. Increasing use of psychology is being made in various spheres of life and extension education is no exception to it. In extension education the change agents deal with the rural people. They teach them the innovations which are expected to change their farms, homes and villages. As stated earlier, the methods used in imparting education are mostly informal and non-formal. Most of the principles and concepts discussed under the title of educational psychology are also applicable to extension educational psychology. The only difference between them is that the former emphasises the educational changes in the children while the latter emphasises the educational changes in rural adults. The main aim in extension education is on utilising the research findings in solving the problems of the rural people. This cannot be done mechanically by developing the physical and economical needs of the people as it may lead to a cultural lag. For attaining permanent changes the values and attitudes of the people should also undergo change. To bring out these changes to suit the changing environment among the rural people is the major concern of the extension educational psychology. Thus the main job of the extension worker is teaching rural people. The knowledge of extension educational psychology will help him in selecting and giving appropriate learning experiences to rural people. These learning experiences are to be given in the area in which the rural people are interested. Human behaviour is always goal-oriented and rural people are no exception to this general rule. If the extension worker helps them in reaching the goals decided by them then they would hear him readily. There are a large number of goals or needs of the rural people which can be arranged hierarchically. The basic needs (e.g., hunger) are more predominant in the life of an individual. An individual tries to satisfy these basic needs and after satisfying them he tries to seek satisfaction of the higher order needs (e.g., prestige). The order of needs from lower (basic) to higher levels include (1) physiological needs (e.g., hunger), (2) safety needs (e.g., security), (3) belonging and love needs (e.g., affection), (4) esteem needs (e.g., prestige), and (5) need for self-actualisation (e.g., desire for self-fulfilment).

The extension worker should understand the basic wants and incentives of the people with whom he has to work. He should relate these needs with his teaching and show the people the way to satisfy them. It is necessary to clarify the relation between these needs and the innovations which would help in satisfying them. The extension worker should identify the personal goals of the people and show them that as a result of learning new things they can attain these goals. Interest in better health for himself and his family may stimulate an individual to learn better family planning practices. The need of money for sending his son for higher education may be an incentive for the farmer to adopt innovations to increase yields. So as a first step, it is necessary to create proper motivation for learning in order to make the extension teaching effective. An individual has to be convinced of the relevance of a thing or action to his own interest, then only we can expect his cooperation.

In extension educational psychology the change agents are more concerned with the adult or grown up people. There is a difference in the behaviour of the adult and the child. The ego of an adult is more developed than that of a child and therefore, he is more sensitive to the social atmosphere around him. The social freedom that an adult enjoys is greater than that which is allowed to a child and therefore, a friendly and congenial atmosphere is more imperative in the education of adults. A child learns ten per cent of his latent potentialities in the average school and completes ninety per cent of his education throughout his life.

An adult is more sensitive to success and failure than a child. He is concerned with the acquisition of mastery over something or is more power hungry. It is, therefore, advisable to allow him occasional experiences which will give him the glow of success. At frequent intervals, it is necessary to point out to him the progress that he has made.

Generally an accepted role is assigned to an adult. Occupation is an integral part of this role. Hence, the extension worker should consider his occupation and acquire entry into his mental world through his occupation. An adult will pick up things more easily if he sees their relationship to his occupation. If he is convinced that he will be able to earn more for himself and his family with the new learning then he will try to learn quickly. This learning related to his vocational interest will be more realistic and long lasting. An adult has a greater sense of responsibility than a child and therefore he should be given some responsibility for his own learning.

There are stronger and more permanent sentiments in the adult than in a child. The extension worker should respect and use these sentiments. The sentiments towards his family, his friends and a strong desire for learning are some of the sentiments which will be of help to the extension worker.

Factors Affecting Adult Learning

In addition to the foregoing there are certain factors which influence the learning of the adults.

1) Age: As an adult passes the stage of maturity there is a decline of interest in sports and active recreation and increase in the sedentary use of leisure. However, some interests do not necessarily diminish in intensity during life, e.g., one's interest in books, newspapers, etc.

2) Environment: An adult living in a poor environment will orient his behaviour towards the attainment of some goals attainable within his environment. He may not have access to some resources from his environment and thus may restrict his behaviour.

3) Political conditions: The policies of the political parties affect our behaviour. The partition of India and Pakistan in 1947 affected the life of many people.

4) Lack of leisure: Apart from learning there are more urgent needs which take up an adult's time. Sleep, looking after the family, the work that earns the family its bread are some of the needs. The more backward the economy of the people the greater is the time that these urgent needs consume. This is one of the reasons for people's backwardness and it creates a vicious circle. However, even in a backward economy people may have leisure. For instance among the agricultural population there are times between the harvesting of a crop and the sowing of the next crop when the farmers can find some time for educational and cultural activities. The extension worker may also try to devise to reduce the drudgery of the people (e.g., use of winnower, etc.) and enable them to snatch more leisure by reducing the time which must be spent on their more urgent needs.

5) Misuse of leisure: The adult may fail to make use of or abuse his leisure. Bad habits are his greatest enemy. Indolence and lethargy rank next to it. They arise due to lack of ambition. It is therefore necessary to educate the people to utilise their time more fruitfully. Time should be considered as

an input for production and should be properly used.

6) Lack of mental peace: An adult is incapacitated from devoting any time to his work and education due to lack of mental peace. If he attends the classes he still cannot concentrate and if he forces himself through the class routine he cannot assimilate his lesson. Social disharmony is one of the enemies of mental peace. This originates in one's social circle. A man may dislike for some reason, the class teacher or his classmates thereby affecting his learning. People in a village quarrel tend to be divided in different parties thereby giving rise to rival factions. This leads to hooliganism and litigation. Even when people are saved from such extremes the whole atmosphere gets vicious and retards improvement. A clean social atmosphere is essential for extension education in which an adult is tolerably free from mental worries.

7) Lack of physical comfort: Constant noises irritate and upset an adult more easily than a child and therefore, the class room should be at a quiet place. As far as possible the adult classes should not be held at places frequented by the public. There should be good light for creating a pleasant atmosphere. The place should also be free from bad odours and should have good ventilation.

8) Lack of meaning: Unless the education imparted has relevance to the everyday life and everyday needs of the adult he will not be enthusiastic to learn it. The learning should be meaningful in showing the connection between the subject matter and his life.

9) Boredom: The span of attention of the rural people is narrow and hence the whole class programme should be planned in accordance with it. An illiterate adult is more easily bored than a man accustomed to education. If education is mixed with recreation then the learning is better in these adults. Hence, it is essential to give as much time to the recreation of adults during class time as to the strictly educational programmes.

To sum up, it is necessary to base the extension educational programmes on the psychology of the rural people (i.e., on their basic interests, urges and capacities) for making them effective.

CHAPTER 3

Communication of Innovations

Communication is essential for social change. Social change is the process by which alteration occurs in the structure and function of a social system. The process of social change consists of three sequential steps, invention, diffusion and consequences. Invention is the process by which new ideas are created or developed. Diffusion is the process by which new ideas are communicated to the members of a social system. Consequences are the changes that occur within a social system as a result of the adoption or rejection of the innovation. Change occurs when a new idea's use or rejection has an effect. Social change is therefore an effect of communication.

THE SMCRE COMMUNICATION MODEL

Communication is the process by which messages are transferred from source to a receiver. In extension education it refers to the process of transferring an idea, skill or aptitude from one person to another accurately and satisfactorily. Failure to communicate successfully has bothered many well-intentioned people. A simple communication model consists of a source (S), message (M), channel (C), receivers (R) and effects of communication (E). One can easily see how communication factors are vitally involved in many aspects of the decision processes which together make up social change. Take a farmer's decision to send his son for higher education, construct a cattle shed or the decision to adopt new improved farming practices. In each of these instances, a message (M) is conveyed to individuals (R) via communication channels (C) from a source individual (S), which causes the receivers to

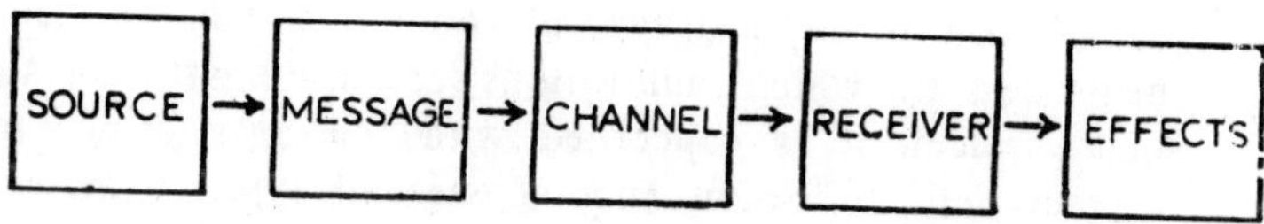

Fig. 3.1 The SMCRE Communication Model.

change an existing behaviour pattern or effect (E) on the receiver (figure 3.1).

1) Source: It is the point of origin of the message. The person who starts the process of communication is also called the communicator. The communicator decides what message is to be sent, how to treat it, what channel to use and which receivers to reach.

2) Message: A message is the information a communicator wishes his audience to receive, understand, accept and act upon. The message may be information, instructions or orders.

3) Channel: It is any thing used by a communicator of messages to connect him with the intended receivers. In extension these are the methods used by the extension workers. It may be a letter, meeting, radio or newspaper through which the communicator reaches the receivers.

4) Receivers: Receivers are the intended audience of messages. They are the consumer of messages. (By acting on the message the receiver is likely to gain economically or socially.) The communicator should identify and aim his messages towards his intended audience.

5) Effect: Effect is the response by the audience to the messages received by them. This may be some kind of mental or physical action. The action should be viewed as a product of the communication process. If it is assumed that a useful message reaches through the means of planned communication to the intended audience, and that they have understood the meaning and intent of the message by interpreting it properly, still the response of the advance to the message needs to be understood. The question that remains then will be the response of the audience to the message—what kind of action took place, by whom and to what extent. The answer to these questions is the effect of the message.

Diffusion is a special type of communication. Diffusion is the process by which innovations spread to the members of a social system. It is concerned with messages of new ideas whereas communication encompasses all types of messages. In diffusion the messages are new and a degree of risk for the receiver is involved. This leads to a somewhat different behaviour on his part in the case of innovations than if he were receiving messages about routine ideas.

Relation between Communication and Diffusion

Crucial elements in the diffusion of new ideas are. (1) the innovation, (2) which is communicated through certain channels, (3) over time, and (4) among the members of a social system. The four elements of diffusion differ only in nomenclature from the essential elements of the SMCRE model, which cited earlier, consists of: (1) source, (2) message, (3) channel. (4) receivers, and (5) effects of communication. This SMCRE communication model closely corresponds to the elements of diffusion: (1) the receivers are the members of social system, (2) channels are the means by which the innovation spreads, (3) the message is a new idea, and (4) the source is the origin of innovation (an inventor, scientist, change agent, opinion leader and the like), and (5) the effects are changes in knowledge, attitude and overt behaviour (adoption or rejection) regarding the innovation. This relationship between the communication and diffusion is shown in figure 3.2.

Characteristics of Innovations

An innovation is an idea, practice or object perceived as new by an individual. It really matters little, as far as human behaviour is concerned, whether or not an idea is objectively new as measured by the amount of time elapsed since its first use or discovery. It is the newness of the idea to the individual that determines his reaction to it.

The speed with which a new idea (innovation) is adopted will depend partly on the characteristics and nature of the idea. Certain farm practices have innate characteristics which speed their rate of adoption, other types may have retarding factors.

1) Cost: New practices that are high in cost generally tend

Elements in SMCRE Model	Source	Message	Channel	Receiver	Effects
Corresponding elements in the diffusion of innovation	Inventors Scientists Change agents or Opinion leaders	Innovation (Perceived attributes such as relative advantage compatibility etc.)	Communication Channels (Mass media or interpersonal media)	Members of a social system	Consequences Overtime 1) Knowledge 2) Attitude Change (Persuasion) 3) Behavioural Change (Adoption or rejection)

Fig. 3.2 Similarity between the Elements in the Diffusion of Innovations and SMCRE Communication Model.

:o be adopted more slowly. The cost of new ideas ranges from ı few paises for certain seed treatment to several thousand rupees 'or farm machinery. The farmers may adopt less costly ideas as t involves less risk.

2) Complexity: New ideas that are relatively simple to ınderstand and use will generally be accepted more quickly than nore complex ideas.

3) Visibility: Practices also vary in the extent to which their peration and results are visible or showy. A new practice will enerally be adopted more quickly if it is visible.

4) Divisibility: Some practices such as the use of fertilisers, : seed varieties may be divided for a comparison of trial results ith the previous practice. However, use of sprayer and certain ther new ideas cannot be easily tried out on a small scale. A ractice that is divisible for trial will generally be adopted more apidly than a practice that is not.

5) Compatibility: A farmer's attitude and values toward a new dea are often affected by his past experience with related ideas. A farmer who has adopted hybrid seed is more likely to adopt ıybrid chickens as he is familiar with the concept of hybrid vigour.

6) Utility: If a new practice is viewed as major improvement over existing methods, it is likely to be adopted rapidly. New crop varieties often produce only a slight improvement over previous varieties. In contrast, hybrid jowar seeds produced an average of 10-15 quintals per acre more than open pollinated varieties.

7) Group action: Some ideas require group adoption, other may be accepted on an entirely individual basis. An individual farmer alone cannot secure electricity for irrigation unless his neighbours are ready to instal pumps on their wells in the beginning.

One of the object of extension efforts is to get new and profitable technologies adopted by the people. This adoption of technologies will result in change which is essential for development. Knowledge and understanding of adoption process shall help the extension workers to speed up the process and increase adoption. Adoption is a decision to make full use of a new idea (innovation) as the best course of action. An individual passes through the adoption process and takes up new ideas and practices. Rejection is a decision not to adopt an innovation. Discontinuance is a decision to cease the use of an innovation after adopting it earlier.

Adoption Process

Adoption is essentially a decision-making process. This decision making process may be divided into sequence of stages with a distinct type of activity occurring during each stage. Similarly, the way in which an individual adopts an innovation is viewed by most researchers as a process. It is a series of related events in a time sequence.

The North Central Rural Sociology Subcommittee for the study of Diffusion of Farm Practices (1955) reviewed the literature and identified five stages of adoption process. The adoption process is the mental process through which an individual passes form first knowledge of an innovation to its final adoption. The five stages conceptualised in this process are (1) Awareness, (2) Interest, (3) Evaluation, (4) Trial, and (5) Adoption. The five stages of the adoption process are described here.

1) Awareness:- At this stage an individual is exposed to an idea but lacks detailed information about it. This is somewhat like seeing something without attaching meaning to it. An individual may know the name a new crop variety but may not know the details of it.

2) Interest :- At this stage an individual is motivated to find out more about the new idea. He seeks more information which will help him to relate the new idea to past experiences and other practices he has used. He wants to know what it is, how it works and what its potential may be. The individual will try to know the details of the new crop variety which he heard at the awareness stage.

3) Evaluation :- Here the individual is concerned with mentally applying the idea to his present or predicted situation. He goes through a sort of mental trial of the new idea. He considers the relative advantages of the new practice over other alternatives. After obtaining the information about the new crop variety an individual will try to relate it to his present circumstances and will think whether he can replace the old variety with the new one.

4) Trial : If the mental trial is favourable then the individual will try to apply the new idea to his particular situation on small scale. He will then seek specific information regarding the technique and method of applying the new idea. The individual will grow the new crop variety on a small scale in order to determine its utility in his own situation. Most of the people will not adopt the new idea without trying it out first on a small scale.

5) Adoption: The individual uses the new idea continuously on a full scale. If the individual is satisfied with the trial, he decides to use the new practice on large scale. In large measure there is satisfaction with the practice. Being satisfied with the trial of the new crop variety an individual adopts it on large scale.

The duration of each of these stages and the length of time between any two stages varies with the personal characteristics of the individual and the nature of the group influences on him.

Rural people obtain information from many sources. Research has shown that sources most used by people vary with the stages in the adoption process. These studies indicate that mass media is most important in attracting awareness and interest while friends and neighbours are first in importance in evaluation, trial and adoption stages.

Innovation and Decision Process

Rogers and Shoemaker (1971) reviewed the "Adoption Process" model. They observed that the stages may not occur in specified order and some of the stages may be skipped. Evaluation occurs throughout the process and the process may not always lead to adoption. There may be rejection also and with more experience and information the innovation which has been adopted may be subsequently be discontinued. They conceptualized it as "Innovation–Decision Process" with few alterations. It is a process through which an individual passes from first knowledge of an innovation, to forming an attitude towards the innovation, to a decision to adopt or reject, to implementation of the new idea and to confirmation of this decision. This process has five stages that occurs overtime and consists of a series of actions. The stages are 1) Knowledge, 2) Persuation, 3) Decision, 4) Implemention, and 5) Confirmation. The functions associated with each stage are described here.

1) Knowledge: An individual is exposed to innovations existence and gains some understanding of how it functions. Knowledge seeking is initiated by an individual and is greatly influenced by his predispositions. Exposure is selective and, generally, an individual tends to expose himself to those ideas which are consistent with his existing attitudes and beliefs, and avoids those which are in conflict with them. Knowing about an innovation is often quite different from using the idea. Most individuals know about the innovations that they have not adopted. The reasons for non-adoption may be their feeling that the innovations are not relevant to their situation and may not be potentially useful. If an individual does not consider the information useful he will not act on it.

2) Persuasion: An individual forms a favourable or unfavourable attitude toward the innovation. Attitude is a positive or negative feeling towards an object that predisposes actions of an individual. Persuasion function is mainly affective or related to feeling. At knowledge stage the mental activity was mainly cognitive (or knowing) but at persuasion stage the mental activity is mainly affective (or feeling). Knowledge of new idea leads to persuasion. In developing a favourable or unfavourable attitude toward the innovation, an individual may mentally apply the new idea to his present or anticipated future situation before deciding whether or not to try it. He tries to know the expected consequences of the innovation. The favourable or unfavourable attitude toward the innovation leads to change in overt behaviour (i.e. adoption or rejection) consistent with the attitude held.

3) Decision: An individual engages in activities which lead to a choice to adopt or reject, the innovation. An individual puts the innovation to a small scale trial in his own situation. Considering the relative advantage, risks involved and many other factors like availability of market, need for the family, resources available etc. the individual takes a decision to adopt or reject the innovation.

4) Implementation: An individual puts the innovation to use in this stage, until this stage the innovation-decision-process is more or less mental exercise. Implementation may involve changes in management of the enterprise and can take place partly before the decision is taken. An innovation is not normally used as such

but is modified by the individual to suit more closely the needs of the person who adopts it. The change or modification made by the user in the innovation to suit his requirement is called reinvention. Reinvention may be good or bad depending on one's point of view. It is difficult to measure the performance of a specific innovation if it changes overtime and across different adopters. The change agents are reluctant to provide on spot guidance by modifying the innovations to meet the requirement of their specific client as it is a skillful and responsible affair. Many times the reinventions made by the users vitiates the very purpose of the innovation. The use of hybrid seed is a good innovation but the reinvention of using the seeds of the hybrid seeds vitiates the purpose of using the hybrid vigour for increasing yields.

5) Confirmation: The individual seeks reinforcement for innovation he has made, but he may reverse his previous decision if exposed to conflicting messages about the innovation. The decision to adopt or reject an innovation is not a terminal act. Human mind is always in a dynamic state and an individual constantly evaluates the situation. If he perceives that the innovation is consistently giving satisfactory or unsatisfactory results, he may continue to adopt or reject the innovation. Discontinuance is a decision to reject the innovation having previously adopted it. An individual may discontinue an innovation after initially adopting it, if the innovation loses its relative advantage or a better substitute is available. A new crop variety due to its superior qualities will replace the old variety which is deteriorated after number of years.

Innovativeness and Adopter Categories

Innovativeness is the degree to which an individual is relatively earlier in adopting new ideas than other members of his social system. Rather than describing Mr. Skeptic as 'less innovative than the average member of his social system' it is handier and more efficient to refer to him as being in the 'late majority' adopter category. This shorthand notation saves words and contributes to clearer understanding as the adopter categories have a great deal in common.

Adopter categories are the classifications of members of a social system on the basis of innovativeness (figure 3.3)

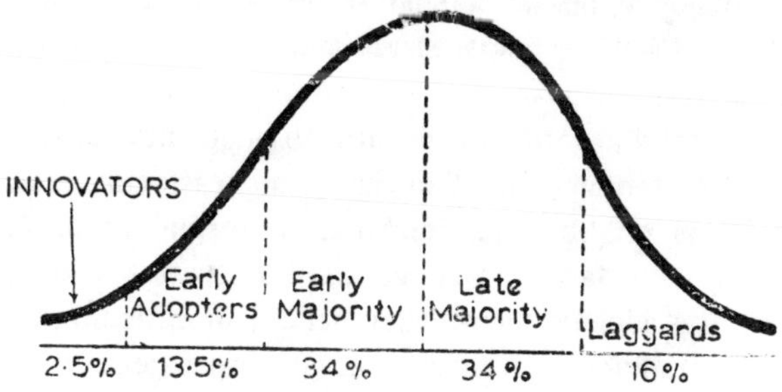

Fig. 3.3 Adopter Categorisation on the Basis of Innovativeness.

All farmers do not adopt a new practice at the same time. Farmers may be classified into five adopter categories according to the relative time at which they adopt a new practice.

1) Innovators: They are the first farmers to adopt a new idea. They are known as experimenters since they try out farm practices before anyone else in their community. They are characterised by large farm size, relatively higher income, high social status, activity in community organisations, access to many sources of information and a ventursome spirit.

2) Early adopters: These follow the motto: "Be not the first by which the new is tried, nor the last to lay the old aside". When compared with the average farmer, the early adopters have slightly higher education, are a little younger in age, and participate more in formal organisations. Their social status is high and they have many informal contacts within the community. They are looked upon as good sources of advice and information by the neighbours. They have more contacts with extension workers.

3) Early majority: These farmers adopt innovations a little earlier than the average farmers. In most respects they are typical of average farmers, their education, farming experience and contacts with extension worker are only slightly higher than that of the average farmers.

4) Late majority: These farmers adopt new ideas just after the average farmers, and have about the same characteristics as the early majority but to a slightly lesser degree. They have slightly less education, social status and extension contacts than the average farmer.

5) Laggards: Laggards are the last to adopt new ideas. They are the oldest farmers and they have the least education, few social contacts and low participation in formal organisations. They resist new farm practices until everyone else in the community has adopted them. They believe in agricultural magic and cling to traditional attitudes. They regard extension workers with negative attitudes and suspicion.

Rate of Adoption

Rate of adoption is the relative speed with which an innovation is adopted by the members of a social system. It is measured by the length of time required for certain percentage of members of a system to adopt an innovation.

The normal rate of progress might require from six to ten years between the introduction of the innovation and its adoption generally throughout the community. An extension worker who understands this can speed up the operation. The trick is to get more informal leaders to become early adopters and more early adopters to become innovators. This can be done when the people have confidence in the extension worker. The extension worker should develop the confidence of the people in him by providing them satisfying experiences.

CHAPTER 4

Extension Teaching Methods

In the communication process extension teaching methods or channels of communication are the tools in the hands of extension workers in transferring new ideas. An extension worker has to deal with many rural people. One of the methods to deal with them is personal visits by the extension worker to the farms or homes of the farmers. A personal visit represents a best learning situation but it may not be always possible to visit the farmers. The extension worker has therefore, to use other teaching methods for reaching the maximum number of people effectively.

SELECTION OF METHODS

The worker must reach more people, reach them more often and keep down the cost per contact. Research studies in extension education show that several methods are better than any one method. The extension worker, therefore, need not try to choose the best method but should use a combination of different methods. The following considerations should be kept in mind while selecting the best combination of methods.

1) The range of methods available to the extension worker.

2) The contribution expected from the method in the programme.

3) Which combination of individuals, group and mass media will be best for a specific plan of work.

4) The length of time the programme will be undertaken in the area.

5) Type of programme to be undertaken, i.e., the type of

information or skills to be imparted.

6) The personality and skills of available extension workers.

7) The type of people to be reached, their sex, age, education, motives and other complex human characteristics need to be understood properly.

8) General local conditions, such as seasonal work, weather conditions, available meeting places, organisation and leadership.

9) Financial and other resources, such as equipment, transport and other facilities in using the method.

Based on the foregoing considerations right methods in the right proportion and at right time should be used. The details of the methods are presented in the following paragraphs.

CLASSIFICATION OF EXTENSION TEACHING METHODS

Extension education is mainly concerned with the dissemination of useful and practical information relating to rural life and helping the rural people in the practical application of such knowledge to rural situations. The extension teaching methods are the means through which the extension worker can achieve this objective. It has been shown by research that extension workers using only one extension teaching method were able to influence a little over one-third of the village families to improve practices in various fields. But where the workers used three methods, including demonstrations, visual aids and the written words, almost two-thirds of the families were influenced to use better practices. Where five methods of teaching were used almost nine out of ten families changed and where nine methods were used 98 per cent of the families were led to change their practices.

Before planning the strategy of extension teaching methods the extension worker should know the details of the methods available for use in the rural situation. From this point of view the extension teaching methods are classified and are presented in the following paragraphs.

I. Extension teaching methods classified according to use of the methods are shown in the following table. Here the methods are grouped according to the number and nature of the contacts inherent in their use.

Individual contacts	Group contacts	Mass contacts
Farm and home visits	Method demonstration meetings	Bulletin Leaflets
Office calls	Leader training meetings	News stories
Telephone calls	Lecture meetings	Circular letters
	Conferences and discussion meetings	Radio
Personal letters	Meetings at result demonstrations	Television
Result demonstrations	Tours Schools Miscellaneous meetings	Exhibits Posters

Indirect Influence

II. The extension teaching methods classified according to form of the methods are as follows:

<table>
<tr><th>Written</th><th>Spoken</th><th>Objective or visual</th></tr>
<tr><td>Bulletins</td><td>General and special meetings</td><td>Result demonstrations</td></tr>
<tr><td>Leaflets</td><td>Farm and home visits</td><td>Exhibits</td></tr>
<tr><td>News articles</td><td>Office calls</td><td>Posters</td></tr>
<tr><td>Personal letters</td><td>Telephone calls</td><td>Motion pictures,</td></tr>
<tr><td>Circular letters</td><td>Radio</td><td>charts, slides and other visual aids.</td></tr>
<tr><td></td><td colspan="2">Method demonstration meetings, meetings at result demonstrations, meeting involving motion pictures and visual aids.
Television</td></tr>
</table>

Indirect Influence

III. While using the foregoing methods the extension worker

uses these methods independently or takes the help of certain audio-visual aids. The word audio-visual aid comprises three words namely:

Audio—refers to sense of hearing
Visual—refers to sense of seeing
Aid—instructional device.

The audio-visual aids are classified in two ways. One is to divide them into the following three categories.

Audio	Visual	Audio-visual
Tape recorder	Flash cards	Cinema projector
Radio	Black board	Television
Recordings	Pictures	Drama

Another method of classification is to divide the aids into projected and non-projected aids.

Projected aids	Non-projected aids
Cinema projector	Flash cards
Slide projector	Flannel graph
Overhead projector	Charts
Opaque projector	Pictures

These are a few of the several ways, in which audio-visual aids can be classified.

Organising Group Discussion

Many of the most important problems can be solved only through cooperative action.

Cooperative group action requires good work from all members. It requires that the cooperating villagers develop the habit of talking, thinking, planning and working as a group.

People become accustomed to group action and become good in group action only by practice. It is the village worker's job to give the villagers every chance to work in cooperative group action.

A well-organised village group discussion conducted properly is the best way to learn cooperative group action. In fact such discussion should be the first step in cooperative effort.

A discussion, properly conducted, requires that each member listens to the ideas of the other members, even though he may not approve of the ideas. This type of discussion should give each member a chance to express his own views.

Members of such groups must learn to put the interest of the group above personal interests.

In democratic group discussion the leadership is shared among the members instead of being held continuously by one person. In this manner all members receive practice in leadership activities. This experience provides a device for the individual development of unselfish leadership that is needed for the success of community development.

As a village discussion group grows and gains confidence it will naturally seek to become a village action group. A village worker must carefully lead the group to see the need for action. Without action villages cannot improve.

In the beginning leadership could be given to discussion. Initiative and most of the knowledge must be provided by the extension worker. Organise the group and help it to gain the skills needed for democratic group action.

The goal will be to see the group eventually attack and solve a common problem without help of extension worker. Joint action is the goal of group discussion.

The first step towards joint action will be getting a small group of villagers to meet and discuss a common problem. If it is difficult to get the villagers to meet as a group, the following suggestions may be helpful:

1) Ask 20 to 25 villagers to meet the extension worker to give advice and guidance on some particular problem.

2) Discover the problem of interest to most villagers and it can become the topic of the first discussion.

Following are general principles about planning and leading the discussion.

1) Prepare for the discussion: Study the problem to be discussed. Think about it in relation to the interest and ideas of the group. Have reference material if possible. Have pictures or charts or any other visual aids that might be useful.

2) Make the group comfortable: People think better if they are comfortable. Be sure, therefore, to select the best meeting place and the most convenient time. Start and finish the meet-

ing on time. Know the name of every member.

3) Seat the group in a circle: Every member of the group should be able to see the faces of all other members. All should remain seated during the discussion. Keep the meeting friendly and informal. See that all take part in the discussion.

4) Allow the group to discuss what the problem really is: If the problem is not clearly defined, try to get it properly defined before the group at the beginning. The leader's opinion must not dominate group opinion. The leader's first job is to bring out ideas of the group members.

5) Discourage speech-makers: Speeches spoil group thinking. Limit any talks to two minutes or less. Stop the speech-maker as tactfully as possible. If the speech-maker is allowed to ramble on he will ruin the discussion. One way to stop him is to say, "Let's hear what someone else thinks about this idea." Asking that all remain seated when talking helps too.

6) All must take part: Often the best thinking is done by people who are too shy to talk. Occasionally, direct questions to these people during the discussion. Show that the answers given by them are good. Never ridicule the ideas of any member of the group. Group discussion is a large conversation. The leader keeps it moving but does not drive it.

7) Guide the discussion group towards action: Get them to the decision and planning stage. This may be done by raising questions and helping them to find facts. Several times during each discussion summarise what has been discussed up to that point.

8) Lead the group to seek technical information and help: The village group will need technical help to solve many problems. Lead them to decide or to consult specialists when a need for this information arises. Try to get the group in the habit of seeking facts. See that members of the group make their own arrangements with specialists or government departments instead of doing this for them.

9) Use visual methods for presenting facts: Introduce new information into the discussion by the use of films, posters, exhibits and demonstrations. Skilful use of visual material will often make a problem so real to villagers that they see the need for action immediately.

10) Use sight-seeing trips to find facts (see tours): Lead the village discussion group to plan trips to other villages where improved practices are being carried out. Good farmers from all villages might be invited to attend the group discussions to give their experiences and ideas.

The preceding general principles if properly used as a guide will help to achieve successful village group discussion. In such discussion groups try to lead the members through the following six steps:

Step 1. Recognising the common problem and becoming seriously concerned about it: Here films, posters, specialists, trips and other methods of presentation of information may have to be used to get the group to recognise the problem. If a problem which is already of serious concern to the group is selected, this step will be unnecessary.

Step 2. Finding the facts to solve the problem: First, get all the facts already known by members of the group brought out in the discussion. When this is done, lead the group to seek facts from literature and specialists. Attempt to develop in the group the habit of making a systematic search for facts when a problem is presented.

Step 3. Analysing the facts: All known facts must be considered in relation to the local problem. Lead the group to examine and test all facts.

Step 4. Reaching a decision to take action: The group decides that it must do something to correct the conditions causing the problem. The decision must be in agreement with the facts discovered by the group.

Step 5. Planning a joint course of action: The plan will provide the answers to who, when, where and how, what material will be needed and how they will be obtained. All these questions must be settled in a joint plan of action.

Step 6. Doing the work: This is the goal of discussion and planning that has gone before. This is the step which builds confidence and enthusiasm. This is the step which draws villagers together in an effective group. Each time the villagers solve a problem by this method they are acquiring the habits of cooperation.

Farm and Home Visit

Farmers are faced with two types of problems that the village worker will be helping with. The type that can be solved best through group action has been treated in the preceding method. The other type is the problem which can be solved by the individual or the family, working alone. Examples of such problems are: better feeding of bullocks, planting better seed, or better sanitation in the home.

In most instances the village worker will have to get individuals to adopt certain simple improved practices before he can expect to achieve village group action.

Getting the villager to improve his methods requires about the same approach as getting a group to adopt an improved method. To convince a farmer that he should plant better seeds, for example, the following steps are necessary:

1) Get acquainted with the farmer.

2) Make friends—don't rush the process—give the villager time to get acquainted with the extension worker.

3) Talk about seeds.

4) Get the farmer to tell his ideas.

5) Tell the farmer new ideas about improved seeds.

6) Show him photographs and give him literature if he is literate.

7) If a demonstration is available, let the farmer see what improved seeds actually will do—if necessary, visit a neighbouring village for this purpose.

8) Get the farmer to agree to try improved seeds.

9) Help him to find out the source for the seeds.

10) Lead him to buy the seeds himself.

11) Help him to decide exactly when and how seeds should be planted.

12) Keep in constant contact with this farmer and give him all additional assistance he needs.

If the extension worker is not certain about any step in an improved practice, don't attempt to advise the farmer. First learn every step and be sure that the information is accurate. If he is asked a question about any problem on which he is working, then his future depends upon giving the right answer. If he does not know the answer, he must go to reliable experts or to rèliable references for help.

Method Demonstration

An extension worker is called on to teach villagers how to do many new kinds of work. When he shows farmers how to do work by doing it himself, he is conducting a method demonstration. The demonstration may be very simple, such as: (1) planting seeds in lines, (2) removing smut from seed, (3) using a mechanical sprayer. Or the demonstration may be more complicated, such as: (1) making soap, (2) drying fruits and vegetables, (3) building a sanitary latrine.

In order to give a successful demonstration one must know perfectly every step in the job. An extension worker must plan the demonstration and practice carefully so that he makes the proper impression on the audience enabling them to learn as quickly as possible.

The demonstration should include what the villagers want to see and what is needed by them at that precise time. For example, don't show villagers how to spray for extermination of insects after the insects have done their damage.

After the extension worker has satisfied himself that he is prepared to give a demonstration and that his information is accurate and complete, he may then take the following action:

1) *Getting Ready*

a) Have village people help him secure a proper place.

b) Decide on the best time.

c) Advertise the event and be sure that enough space is available so that everybody can see.

d) Get all the necessary equipment well ahead of time. Getting ready often takes longer than giving the demonstration.

2) *Presentation*

The presentation will be interesting if the chosen subject is of interest to the people. In giving the demonstration try to act naturally. Be at ease. When talking, stand erect and look at the audience.

Talk clearly and loud enough to be heard. This is important.

Be enthusiastic. Enjoy doing the job. Be friendly.

The steps in the actual demonstration are as follows:

1) Tell the villagers what you are going to do.

2) Tell them why you are doing the job.

3) Show the villagers how to do the job.

4) Then let willing villagers do the job.

5) Allow all villagers who are interested to do the job as long as time and interest permits.

6) Correct mistakes politely.

7) Encourage questions and answer them thoroughly.

If the extension worker does not know the answer to any question say that he does not know but that he will find out. Make it a point later to get the answer for those that are interested.

The method demonstration is one of the village workers' best devices. No village worker can feel that he is doing his job unless he shows villagers how to do things by new and improved ways.

After a demonstration the village worker should make it easy for villagers to adopt the new practice. He should also help them to obtain the necessary equipment or material. He should be available for any additional information needed by the villagers. Written instructions or a leaflet explaining the process should be left with the villagers who may use the new practice.

The measure of a successful method demonstration is the number of people who adopt the new method. Briefly, in a method demonstration do the following things:

1) Demonstrate a new method which will help the villagers.

2) Demonstrate equipment and material which are available.

3) Prepare well for demonstration.

4) Collect all equipment and material needed for the demonstration.

5) Tell the villagers the time and place and subject of the demonstration.

6) Lead the villagers who want to learn the new method.

7) Show them how to do the new work.

8) Get them to try the new work.

9) Correct mistakes and have villagers practise the new method.

10) Fit the new method into a definite plan for village improvement.

In giving method demonstrations show the farmers how the job is done. The extension worker must not hire labour to show the improved ways. No teacher is a good teacher unless he is prepared to practise what he teaches.

Result Demonstration

A result demonstration is a way of showing people the value of an improved practice. This is done by comparing the improved and the old practice so that villagers may see and judge results for themselves. This way may be used by the village worker to teach villagers the value of practices such as: (1) Using improved seed, (2) Anti-malarial measures, (3) Using improved plough, (4) Using fertiliser, and (5) Using improved cultural methods.

To be successful in the use of result demonstration the extension worker must demonstrate only those practices which he thinks are good and which are based on a real need of the villagers. Before selecting a practice for demonstration the village worker should:

1) Ask an expert if the practice will work well in the village.

2) Discuss the practice with the villagers.

3) Find out if villagers already know the value of the practice.

4) Find out if they are interested in the new practice.

After the extension worker decides to demonstrate a new practice he selects one or more villagers to conduct demonstrations. Select a demonstrator who has the confidence and respect of his neighbours, and who is interested in improving his methods.

The extension worker should visit his demonstrator in the beginning and plan the demonstration. In the beginning a demonstrator should be asked to demonstrate only one practice at a time. He should select plots which can be seen easily by villagers. He should measure those plots so that equal areas of land side-by-side can be used. One area will show the old way, the other area will show the new way. After you have worked with the demonstrator and are satisfied with the plans, take the following steps.

1) Get all necessary material and equipment ready.

2) Have village people present when demonstration begins.

3) Begin keeping records.

4) Mark demonstration plots with large signs so all can see as they pass.

This is only the beginning of the demonstration. The following steps must be taken in order to complete the job:

1) Make a calendar of all work that must be done.

2) Visit the demonstration often to see that plans are being carried out properly.

3) If the demonstration is succeeding, give publicity to the demonstrator.

When the time arrives and results can be seen:

1) Conduct tours to the demonstration.

2) Let the village demonstrator do the talking.

3) Make a summary of the records.

4) Give publicity to the results.

5) Get other farmers to agree to demonstrate during the next season.

6) Get as many farmers as possible to try the new practice.

One way to get villagers to try the new practice is to have them present when crops are harvested and have them help measure the results. This will dispel doubt as to the actual result of the new practice.

These results may also be used in neighbouring villages in teaching other cultivators. Charts can be made of the demonstration results and carried to other villages along with photographs showing the comparisons. The best method is to have neighbouring villagers visit the result demonstration.

The Newspaper

All newspapers and other periodicals reaching the villages should be used as much as possible.

Material that will appear in these papers does not have to be news. Many papers or periodicals going to villagers welcome the 'service-type' information. This is the main type of message that one has to transfer. Extension work occasionally makes news that the newspapers will want to use, more often extension worker will place in the papers stories that are not news.

It is well, however, to give anything one write the 'news

slant'. For example, if extension worker believes that a locust invasion is likely, he will write a story on what local farmers should do when the locusts come. To do this, he will outline each step that must be taken by the farmer in order to protect his crops and the community from these insects. He will make this story more interesting by pointing out in the first paragraph that locusts are likely to come in the very near future. Tell the source of the information. When preparing a story follow these rules:

Write a simple story that is

1) Easy to understand,

2) In the language of the village people, who are reading the story,

3) Accurate in all details, and

4) In short sentences and paragraphs.

Most of the stories will be the 'how-to-do-it' type. Tell the story by telling how some local villagers succeeded with the improved job or practice.

In any event, all stories that one prepares for the papers will be written to help people in villages. In rare cases write a story which will simply report community activities. Even in this case the activities will have helped to solve some village problem.

Get acquainted with the editors of all the papers coming in villages.

If extension worker thinks, that it is impossible for him to prepare stories for the paper, tell the editor what the problems are. He will most likely assure that writing for the newspaper is not difficult.

After getting acquainted with editor or editors and receiving his promise that he would be interested in the material, prepare a brief story and let him look at it. If he does not accept the story and is a man interested in serving his readers, he will tell you why he cannot accept it. He will tell you how you can prepare another story that he will accept.

It is almost always true that after a short period of introduction, alert newspaper people will seek the extension worker and insist that he continue giving material for the papers. Sometimes the editor becomes so interested that he will prepare much of the material himself. In the beginning, however, the extension worker must take the initiative.

Does the extension worker work in villages that do not have enough newspapers? If so, he will be doing a service to people by introducing some good rural papers. There are newspapers written in simple local language that can help the extension worker do his job better.

Leaflets and Pamphlets

Literature is the basis of any teaching programme. In extension teaching simple leaflets and pamphlets are valuable and essential tools in the hands of the intelligent extension worker. The leaflet, is a single sheet of paper folded to make a four page piece of printed matter. However, a leaflet can be printed on one side or printed on two sides of a folded sheet, or folded three or four times with printing on all sides. The leaflet usually treats one job or one small problem. The best leaflets give accurate and specific instructions on how to do a job. A pamphlet or bulletin, on the other hand, may contain many pages and treat a number of topics or steps in a given problem. The best pamphlets are brief and simple.

Obtain as many pieces of literature as possible for use and reference. Secure many copies of the same circular or leaflet for passing them to interested villagers.

If it is possible to print leaflets for use in the village, follow these rules:

1) Write on one simple idea such as fertilising sugar cane, or using the best wheat seed, or selecting laying hens, or building a kitchen shelf.

2) Write on those subjects or jobs that are of interest to the villager.

3) Write in the villager's language.

4) Use simple words and short sentences.

5) Use short paragraphs and don't crowd material on a page.

6) Use illustrations and pictures which are easily understood.

7) Give complete instructions.

8) Check instructions for accuracy.

9) Write sentences not over 15 words.

10) Write average sentence having ten words or less.

11) Most of the words in each sentence should be one syllable. Few words, if any, should be over two syllables.

It is hard to write for easy reading. But the easier the writing, the more it will be read. This has been proven in many reading tests.

Circular Letters

Circular letter is one of the best teaching devices. This is a letter which is reproduced and sent with the same information to many people. To even partly literate villagers, receiving a letter can be very important. Receiving such mail will have great influence. However, the value of a letter will depend mostly on how well it is written.

The best letters will:

1) Be brief
2) Be simple
3) Have a single purpose
4) Be part of the programme or campaign
5) Be clear
6) Have complete information
7) Lead to action.

Circular letters can teach and also save the time of the extension worker. They can be inexpensive if their production and despatch is planned properly. If extension worker cannot get a cyclostyling machine, enlist the assistance of the school master. He can allow his students to copy the letter and pass them out to the villagers.

Such letters must have a personal touch, short sentences and short paragraphs.

The personal touch arouses interest. Each letter must arouse interest. There are other ways, however, to interest the reader. If possible, this interest should be aroused in the first sentence.

An example of a circular letter follows:

"Dear Friend:

In our meeting last week as you will recall, we discussed controlling mosquitoes. A number of suggestions were made. One suggestion was to clean the tank and place young fish in the tank. These fish will eat mosquito eggs. In this way we may control malaria. Your committee has decided to meet again next Friday at seven o'clock. At this meeting we will discuss ways to clean the tank. Would you come and give us your ideas?

(Signed) Village worker."

If circular letter proves popular, it may always be expedited. It may be published weekly or fortnightly. This type of letter would contain news and announcements as well as how-to-do-it stories. To publish a regular letter, one must organise production. It must be organised cheaply enough to finance easily. Distribution must be fast and cheap also. This can be done by cooperative effort.

Blackboards

The blackboard is helpful in meetings and group discussions. Chalk and some kind of an eraser is all the equipment needed.

Prepare a blackboard with a piece of plywood about 30 by 40 inches. Paint this board with blackboard paint. To carry the board from village to village, make it in two pieces and hinge it in the middle. Have a small strip of wood attached to the inside of the fold so it can be slid across the board after it is opened and make the board firm.

While conducting meetings of discussions, write the topic for discussion on the board. In most cases this topic should be in the form of a question. Example: "What is the best way to get the village tank cleaned?"

During the discussion place under the written question the suggested answers offered by the group. Also place on the board the suggestions given by the expert.

By writing on the board in this manner one can hold the attention of the group. One can also keep their attention on the particular subject being discussed. It is good to put drawings on the board to illustrate points.

The following rules in using the blackboard may be observed:

1) Have it clean
2) Use clean eraser
3) Write in large letters
4) Don't talk as you write
5) Face group after writing and continue the discussion
6) Don't fill the board

7) Don't use abbreviations
8) Keep drawings simple
9) Use coloured chalk; yellow chalk is good at night
10) Don't stand in front of the blackboard, stand to one side
11) Practise using the blackboard.

For conducting literacy classes, the blackboard is very useful.

Photographs

Photographs are especially suited to teaching illiterates. They are useful also in illustrating written material. Everybody likes to see a photograph of himself best of all. If extension worker can afford to buy any equipment, one of the first things he should buy is a camera.

A good way to use photographs is to place them on a village bulletin board.

1) Arrange them to tell a story, or
2) Tell the steps in an improved practice
3) Giving accurate details, or
4) Show before and after results.

Good photographs used in this manner:

1) Show action
2) Show emotion
3) Show people as they really are
4) Are easily understood.

People love photographs and will become attached to the extension worker who can produce them and who will use them. But some photographs are a waste. They have little value if:

1) They are not lively
2) They are not arranged to teach
3) They are not clear
4) They are dirty
5) They are too small
6) They are in bad taste.

Posters

The poster is an important visual aid. But like other 'aids' the poster is never used alone. It must always be part of a campaign or a teaching programme. It will serve first to inspire the people. It will prove to villagers that there is official interest in the problem treated. Lastly, as long as it remains in the village it will serve as a reminder to the villager.

A good poster arouses people's interest. It makes them feel a part of the work at hand.

To be useful a poster must be planned for a special job. It must be planned for the people who are supposed to do the job.

The following points should be considered in making a poster:

1) To do a special job

a) Promote one point (example: kill flies, manure paddy),

b) Support local demonstrations,

c) Support local exhibits.

2) To be planned for the people who are supposed to do the job:

a) Common dramatic pictures that will stop people and make them lock,

b) Tell the story in a single glance,

1) Have few words

2) Have simple words

3) Have one idea

4) Have bold letters,

c) Must picture everyday living,

d) Should be in pleasing colours,

e) Should be at least 20 by 30 inches in size.

f) Must be timely.

Generally speaking a poster should contain three main divisions. The first part usually announces the purpose of a project. The second sets out conditions. The third recommends action. Each of these three main divisions may be illustrated with striking art supported by brief language.

Posters that are produced properly are often not effective because they are put in a poor place or not posted. Posters should be placed where people pass or placed where people gather.

Some posters fail to do good because they are not followed with other devices such as meetings, demonstrations, and films.

A poster must be part of a campaign as a poster will not stand alone.

Flash Cards

Flash cards are used in the same way as filmstrips. In flash cards, however, people see the picture directly, instead of seeing it on a screen. The story is told as each card is held before the group. The story is simple and tells about one thing. It may be on mosquito control, how to make hay or how to clean dishes.

Flash cards should:

1) Be used in groups of not over 30 people.

2) Be large enough for everyone to see—at least 22 by 28 inches.

3) Be simple line drawings or photographs, or cartoons.

4) Be adapted to local conditions.

5) Have plenty of colour.

It is best to limit the number of flash cards to 10 or 12 for one talk. In order to plan the most effective cards, talk on the main ideas that you want villagers to remember. Prepare a picture for each idea which will give visual impact to the idea.

To teach well with flashcards:

1) The story on each card must be familiar.

2) Must use simple words and local expressions.

3) Must bring in local names of people and villages.

4) Must hold cards so people can see clearly.

5) Must hold cards against body and not up in air (turn body toward the different parts of the group to show cards to all the group).

6) Glance down at card as you tell the story.

7) Point to important objects without covering the card with hand.

8) Be enthusiastic and enjoy telling the story.

Stack the cards in order. As one card is finished it is slid behind the other so that it will be in order the next time it is used.

After teaching by flash cards let the people participate in the discussion or telling the story. It is a better discussion or better story if they participate. If anyone in the group is good at telling the story or leading a discussion, let him take the cards and use them with other groups.

Flannelgraph

A flannelgraph is pieces of flannel or sandpaper stuck on flannel. Just press pieces against a background of flannel and they will stay there until they are removed. If scraps of sandpaper are pasted to the backs of photographs, these photographs will cling to a large piece of flannel. The same is true when sandpaper is stuck to the back of drawings or lettering on medium-weight paper. Even illustrations from magazines can be used for this purpose.

A 30 by 40 inch piece of flannel should be large enough for any audience you will have. A good grade of cotton flannel with thick nap is best. In preparing a flannelgraph story do the following:

1) Place the title of your story in large letters at the top of the flannelgraph (a background flannel will be stretched tightly and fastened securely to a stand or board for receiving the story).

2) Prepare a story in drawings, photographs or printed illustrations.

3) Cut these from their paper background and paste pieces of sandpaper on their backs. (Sandpaper strips an inch or so wide should be stuck at intervals of several inches. A medium or coarse grain sandpaper will work best.)

4) Keep the story simple.

5) The illustrations should be big and bold. This is true also of lettering.

It is a good idea to arrange each part in the order it will be added to the board. These parts may be numbered on the back.

Flannelgraph is well adapted for the 'build-up' story. The clever user can place interesting pieces on the flannel and keep the audience wondering how the story will end until the final piece is placed. The capacity for build-up and suspense is this medium's best advantage.

Films

People who will not attend any kind of meetings will go to see films. Because of this, films are one of the most effective means of arousing interest. They are good for teaching. As long as good teaching films are scarce, films should be used primarily to get people to attend meetings.

Good films are used:

1) To arouse interest and change attitudes.

2) To present facts in an interesting way.

3) To bring new practices to a village in a short time.
4) To reach illiterate as well as literate people.

A film has the following advantages:

1) A complete process can be shown in a short time.
2) People identify themselves with those in the picture.

In selecting films for showing, try to select those that are:

1) Simple
2) Direct
3) Interesting
4) Timely
5) Personal.

As a general rule, give a short talk before a picture is shown, explaining the purpose of the meeting and of the picture. However, most good pictures are self-contained. More important, after the picture, is to allow the villagers to discuss and to ask questions.

The moving picture should not be used alone. It should be used in connection with a definite programme or campaign. It should be supplemented with literature, posters, demonstrations and discussions. It should lead to action.

Slides

Most filmstrip projectors will show slides. Slides are used in the same way as the filmstrip.

The difference is:

1) Slides are single pictures usually in colour.
2) Slides are in a cardboard frame.

A set of coloured slides is useful teaching device.

Arrange to get coloured film and make slides. With these slides tell the story of achievements in the village. A 35 mm camera is necessary for making slides that fit most projectors.

One way to get slides of local activities is to get a camera on a cooperative basis and arrange finance for buying film.

Filmstrips

A filmstrip is a series of still pictures on one roll. These pictures are arranged together in such an order that they will tell a story or they will explain the steps of an improved practice. Show filmstrips through a filmstrip projector. There are filmstrip projectors that do not require electricity.

The use of filmstrips is one of the best ways to teach improved methods because:

1) The machines are simple to operate.

2) The pictures can be held on the screen for a long time.

3) The extension worker with a camera can take good pictures of local practices and have them made into a filmstrip at very little expense.

4) The filmstrip and projector take little space and can be carried easily.

5) The villagers can participate through discussions on each picture.

Filmstrips have this additional advantage. A complete process such as growing paddy can be shown at one short session.

Specimens, Models and Exhibits

The best place to study about a new crop is where the crop is grown. Sometimes this is impossible. The next best thing is to bring specimens of the crop to the meeting. By doing this farmers see the plant, see how tall it grows and examine its seeds and root system.

How many such specimens can be used in teaching will depend on how resourceful extension worker is. Keep the need for such specimens in mind and collect all that would seem to be helpful.

The best way to prepare samples of small crops, such as grasses and legumes, is to mount the specimens on sheets of thin cardboard. Mount them by tying them to the cardboard with thread or string. Attach a caption plainly printed to each cardboard.

Models of many agricultural items can be helpful in teaching. Models of new farm equipment, houses, compost pits, and sanitation devices all have their advantages.

Demonstrations with models or specimens do not substitute for actual demonstrations in the field. Demonstrations in the field are always better.

One of the best placed to get over the message to the largest number of people is at melas or fairs. An exhibit placed in such big gatherings will reach large numbers in a short time.

Because people are passing rapidly, such exhibits must be

well prepared. The message must be understood in the short time it takes people to walk by the exhibit.

In planning such exhibits remember the following points:

1) Limit to one idea
2) Make it simple
3) Make it large
4) Make it timely
5) Make it durable
6) Make it attractive.

Other points to remember are:

1) Use too few rather than too many items.
2) Use bold, simple, bright letters and figures.
3) Label all parts which need explanation.

The best exhibits are those that tell a story. Good exhibits tell the story without the need for an attendant.

After arranging the exhibit, ask some disinterested person to study it. If this person can tell the story put across the exhibit then it is likely to succeed. If not, it would be a good idea to adjust the exhibit for easier understanding.

During the mela or fair, study the people who pass the exhibit. The lesson learned from these people will assist in mounting another exhibit at the next mela.

If the people stop and spend time in studying the message, feel sure that proper approach is adopted. If people understand the exhibit it has been a success. Do not hesitate to discuss the exhibit with a cross-section of people. This is the only way to improve the presentation.

It is always better to exhibit the real item than a model. To show a new plough, exhibit the plough itself, then follow this exhibit with a demonstration.

Radio Talks

Radio, as everybody knows, is a very good information tool. It is a mass medium of conversation and can reach large numbers of people at any given time.

Every radio station, is broadcasting several varieties of useful talks by eminent scientists and extension specialists in the fields of agriculture, animal husbandry, etc., for rural people. While some talks appear very interesting certain other talks are felt to be dull and drab. Experience shows that many tal belong to the latter category. Is it due to the defective script writing or talking or listening? Since radio talks play an important role in the life of nation, it is worthwhile examining this issue. Nation has pledged for the betterment of rural villages, particularly with reference to present day food crisis and the necessity for increased agricultural production.

Nature and Potentialities of the Medium

The radio belongs to the spoken word means of communication. The medium is transient and fleeting and its impression is quick and faint. It is a one way communication. The message has to be simple and clear so that people can understand it and act. The broadcaster has to get and hold the attention of the audience, otherwise the message is lost.

Radio can inform about past, present, or future activity. It stimulates curiosity on the part of the listener. The interest of the intended audience can be aroused and built up. It can create desire to see, hear and act. It can widen horizons and mental outlook, break down prejudices and bring enlightenment. It can promote favourable attitudes and influence emotions. It can inspire the listeners to some form of action. It may help in guiding the listeners' interests and to grasp the significance of new ideas and thoughts. It can interpret policies.

Radio as a medium can be popular, pleasing and even exciting, but it cannot be used for the task of conveying heavy and detailed knowledge. It can be used for:

1) Announcements.
2) Intimation or information regarding availability of materials, prices, places etc.
3) Warnings relating to weather, outbreaks of diseases, pests.
4) Seasonal hints.
5) News stories.
6) News reviews—about farmers and farming.
7) Interviews.
8) Questions and answers.
9) Short talks.
10) Plays, sketches, ballads, burrkathas etc.
11) Features.

12) Documentaries.

There are certain special advantages of the radio as a medium. It reaches more people more quickly than any other means of mass communication. It is relatively cheap. It reaches illiterate audiences also. It builds enthusiasm and maintains interest.

This medium has its own limitations too. The broadcasting facilities are available only in limited places. The time assigned for the talks is usually limited. It is difficult to check on results. Only skilled personnel can handle the broadcasting. There are not enough sets in the rural areas. Its influence is limited to people who can listen intelligently. The programmes for rural people frequently lose out in competition with entertainment.

Nature of the Rural Listeners

It is necessary to know the general psychology of rural listeners who are mostly adults. The adults have less physical energy than young people, are mentally a little less quick and adjust less easily to new situations, are more set in their attitudes, desire security more than adventure, are less reckless and more thoughtful of consequences and (sometimes, at least) more tolerant and more wise.

All the rural listeners may or may not be educated in the formal sense. Farmers do strenuous work throughout the day and like everyone else, would rather be entertained than educated after a day's hard work. Most of them do not take notes while listening to a programme. They value the radio as a source of news and other information, as a source of entertainment and company. They may not like to follow lengthy programmes unless the programmes hold exceptional interest. The rural listeners do not constitute a uniform type of audience. There are differences in education, age, income, experience, etc. The receptivity of the listeners to the programme depends upon their background and thus varies with the individuals. They have more interest in items of direct, timely and local interest to them. Many of them are faced with several problems and always in a mood to look forward to solutions for problems such as lack of food, clothing, housing, employment, health, etc. They try to stick up to their traditions, customs and culture.

Preparation of Script for Talk

Before proceeding with writing there are several preliminary considerations to be made:

1) Determine the purpose first. The objective should be clear.

2) Know the type of listeners to be informed.

3) Decide the method of presentation of the information whether it is straight talk, interview or panel discussion, etc.

4) Collect all the possible related material helpful for writing.

5) Select authentic material and arrange it in order.

6) Be sure to include supporting and illustrative facts.

After keeping the required material ready, one can start writing. There are, again, several factors to be considered while writing:

1) Remember that it is writing for the ear only. Listener cannot stop the speaker and ask something which he has missed. The way a script sounds is far more important than the way it looks and reads. Write as one talks and think of how the writing sounds.

2) Avoid an academic style. Use simple and familiar language having an informal approach. Avoid jaw breaking words. Mix short and medium length sentences for variety.

3) Prefer to use local information and the experience of farmers, even their names can be included.

4) Keep listeners' viewpoint in mind at all times.

5) Make listeners realise the importance of the programme.

6) Be direct and personal.

7) Use statistics sparingly.

8) Be humorous.

9) Time the script. Talk it aloud and time it accordingly. For a 10 minute programme, the talk time may be about nine minutes.

Another important aspect is that the script has to be divided into different parts depending upon the nature of the message to be conveyed. The following parts may constitute an effective script dealing with an improved agricultural practice:

1) The first part should be designed to attract the attention of the listeners towards the subject proper. A strong opening makes people want to listen.

2) The second part may analyse the present situation, laying special emphasis on the problems encountered based on local needs.

3) The third part may give out facts about the recommended practice and its merits over the previous practices and try to win the confidence of the listener.

4) The fourth section may deal with an appeal to action.

5) Finally the script may end with a summarisation of all the different parts. This will give an opportunity for the listener to know all important ideas in the talk again and act as reinforcement.

Presentation of Talk

However excellent the written script may be it is the delivery of the talk that matters. The listener is concerned with the talker only and the talker is the person who communicates. Experience with radio talk programmes has shown that unfortunately most persons read the script and do not talk, at least it sounds that way. The following factors may be useful in making talks communicative:

1) Be yourself: Feel free and easy in front of the microphone. Rehearse in front of the mike and this will help in developing confidence.

2) Just talk to the people and don't read: Speak naturally. Don't spend any time worrying about the voice. Keep the voice down to the living room level, as if you are conversing with any of your farmer friends. Talk along at a normal rate. In ordinary conversation you change pace once in a while, and it is a good idea to do that with a radio talk.

3) Observe mike manners: Turn aside from the mike if you have to cough or clear your throat. Try to avoid noisy breathing. Don't turn your head from side to side, since that makes your voice fade as it comes through the mike.

4) Be enthusiastic: Put a smile in your voice and talk with pleasant enthusiasm.

5) See that the close of the programme is strong and friendly and natural but not hurried.

6) Let the whole programme, from start to finish be in time. It is unpleasant to the radio station staff either if you run short of material or keep on talking after your time is up.

7) Let your personality shine through your programme by giving personal touches, references, human interest angles, etc.

Slide and/or Filmstrip Projector

There are many makes of projectors available and although individual features vary, the fundamental principle of direct projection is used in these projectors irrespective of size and light output.

The rays of light directly come from the projection bulb or source of light, pass through condenser lenses, the object (may be filmstrip or slide), the objective lenses (they are also called focussing lenses), and finally the enlarged image appears on the screen.

The following steps are necessary in operating a slide/filmstrip projector.

1) Set the projector on the stand and connect the cord.

2) Obtain the appropriate image on the screen and adjust it in appropriate position by tilting and moving the machine forwards or backwards as required.

3) Focus the light beam on the screen to sharpen the edges of white light area.

4) Insert the strip slide in the carrier as per directions of the makers. First read the filmstrip title, turn the strip head down, push the strip into the channel and turn the operating knob.

5) The frame on the screen should be focussed sharp. If it is split between two frames then adjust it to one by adjusting the framing control.

6) Operate the filmstrip at the desired speed.

Opaque Projector

The opaque projector is also known as the episcope. It permits non-transparent materials such as flat pictures, book illustrations, tables, drawings, photographs and even certain specimens and objects to be shown on a screen for group observations.

The opaque projector works on the principle of reflecting light from an opaque surface to the screen. The flat picture which is to be shown on screen is placed in the projector through an opening of about 6″ × 6″. A strong light from the projector lamp is thrown on this picture and the picture is reflected on a screen with the help of mirrors. The screen image is normally less brilliant than in the case of a slide or other transparency where light passes directly through the picture.

The following steps are necessary in operating the projector.

1) Place the projector on the stand and connect the power cord.

2) Turn on lamp.

3) Turn on motor for cooling system (if cooling system is there).

4) Place the material on plate. As the operator faces the screen, materials are placed on the plate face up, with the bottom of the picture towards screen. Exercise great care when using books in opaque projector. Pages must be flat. Avoid damage when inserting and removing books.

5) Bring image to sharp focus by turning lens left or right. Move the projector towards or away from the screen to obtain satisfactory picture size.

6) Operating the opaque projector involves only proper insertion of materials in the desired sequence.

7) After showing material turn off the lamp and then turn off fan.

Overhead Projector

The overhead projector projects an image from a slide or transparency back over the operator's shoulder to a screen. Rays of light are reflected upward to a projection stage and onto an objective lens, which is centrally supported above the stage. The light strikes a mirror and is reflected to a screen located at the back of the operator. The lens and the mirror stand above the machine in periscope fashion. The machine may rest on the teacher's table or it may be on the projection stand. The teacher may sit or stand before the class.

The advantage of the overhead projector is that the teacher can always face the class. The illuminated image is visible in a darkened room. The teacher can operate the projector while teaching and hence no extra projectionist is required. The following steps are necessary in operating the overhead projector.

1) Place the projector at the front of the room with the focussing lens facing the screen and approximately two metres away from the screen.

2) Turn on the switch.

3) Place the transparency on the glass top in proper position.

4) Adjust the projector lens till the image is sharp and in focus.

5) While writing on the transparency be careful in not obstructing the view with your hand.

6) Switch off the lamp whenever the projection is not required and let the fan run. This will help in increasing the lamp life and keeping the projector cool.

7) Before switching off the projector ensure that cool air comes out of the exhaust fan to indicate that the lamp and the interior of the projector have been cooled.

Movie Projector

The movie projector is an instrument through which motion pictures are projected. A motion picture is a series of still pictures taken in rapid succession, developed and finally projected as a series of still pictures, but under such conditions as to give the viewer an illusion of motion.

The motion picture film is divided into two parts.

The Picture Track

The motion picture camera, actually a device for recording a series of still pictures at the rate of 24 exposures per second, is set into operation. This happens because the motion-picture camera rapidly 'snaps' 24 still pictures or frames per second (16 frames for silent motion pictures). When these 'still frames' are projected or flashed in a sequence on a screen, the impression of life and motion is apparent to the viewer. Because the normal eye is not constructed to detect these brief light intervals of length 1/50 of a second, but is rather influenced by the persistence of the image, the mind gains the impression that the screen is continuously lighted. Since the eye cannot detect when one picture is replaced by the next, a visual mental impression of motion is received in the brain. Thus the illusion of motion arises from what in reality is a rapidly changing sequence of still pictures.

The Sound Track

Sound is photographed on the photographic film. The photographic negative pictures and sound are then printed on one positive by ordinary photographic processes. The resulting film, when run through a modern sound projector, gives rise to the audio-visual impression that is called a 'sound motion-picture'. When the sound for a motion-picture film is photographed, the sound waves are picked up by a microphone which converts the varying sound waves into similarly varying patterns of electric current.

The means by which sound is reproduced from a sound motion-picture film is practically the reverse of the way it is recorded. As the film moves through the sound motion picture projector, a light of constant intensity is directed through the sound track on the film. The light passes through the track in lesser or greater amount depending on the light variation in the sound track. This residual variable light is directed towards a photo electric cell which converts the variable intensities into similarly varying electric currents. There, in turn it sets up corresponding movements in the loudspeaker diaphragm. Thus, the original sounds recorded when the sound track of the film was made are once again reproduced.

It is necessary for the extension worker to know the working of the projector. Effective use of motion-pictures requires planning and preparation. Some guidelines are provided here to help the extension worker in the use of films.

Know the tools in detail so that one is familiar with projection equipment.

Projectors

Different types of motion-picture projectors are: 70 mm; 35 mm; and 8 mm. However, 16 mm projector is best suitable for class room teaching. Bell and Howell, Victor, RCA,

Photophone, etc., are among the many different 16 mm motion picture projectors. Each has distinct characteristics and advantages but works on similar principle. It is necessary to know different parts of these projectors and their procedure of handling.

Screens

Screen is to provide maximum possible visibility of the image with minimum glare or strain on the eyes. Different screens are used for different purposes.

a) Beaded screen: projected in long narrow rooms.

b) Matted screen: suited in wide rooms like auditoriums.

c) Aluminium or silver screen: used for astero-pictures, colour slides or films.

d) Lenticular screen: useful for semi-darkened rooms.

e) Improvised screen: A rectangular piece of white cloth is fixed on the wall or a white washed wall is used as a screen.

Selection and Preview of Film

The film should be selected taking the audience into account. It should be suited to the occasion. The film should be projected and previewed by the extension worker. Key points to be discussed with learners before and after the screening of the film should be noted.

Screening the Film

There should be proper seating, light and darkening facilities. The learners should be prepared before the film is screened by arousing their curiosity and asking them to note some of the key ideas. After the film is screened the key ideas should be discussed with the viewers.

Tape Recorder

The tape recorder is an audio aid or instrumental device by which the recordings are made and are again played when desired. The recording is done on magnetic tape. It is like a ribbon 1/4" wide usually made of plastic but in some cases paper is used. This plastic or paper is coated with a very finely ground iron oxide material. This material is pigmented on the tape. These tapes are reeled in spools. The tape recorder accommodates two spools, one empty take up spool and the other containing tape for recording or playing back as the case may be. Iron oxide has magnetic property, i.e., it can be magnetised by an electric field when brought in contact with it. So while recording the chemical reactions take place on the tape and the sound is recorded. The tape recorder automatically erases the old recording while making the new recording.

If the tape is stored under normal room temperature and humidity it is not erased but holds sharp, clear quality for many years.

Tape, Speeds and Tracks

Two-track, four-track and one-track tape recorders are available. Four-track recorders are more complicated in use, and four-track recordings cannot be played on two-track machines if all the four-tracks have been utilised. It is now standard practice to make all the recordings from left to right.

Although a four-track machine may seem to be more useful, a careful note must be made of the contents of each track to avoid any confusion. For field work, a two-track machine is simpler to use and may cost less than a four-track machine of comparable quality.

As the quality of both tape-recording heads and drive motors have been improved, the need to use different speeds for special purposes has diminished. A tape speed of 9.5 cm ($3\frac{3}{4}''$) per second is now the accepted form for non-professional recordings. However some battery recorders still run at half of this speed for reasons of economy.

The development of battery-powered tape recorders has extended the possible applications of these machines to field work. There is no need for heavy batteries and voltage conversion equipment. A few torch batteries of the common type are all that is required to power a recorder capable of a satisfactory standard of performance. The following points may be considered for its effective use in education and training:

1) Tape messages from notable persons, holding high rank in public life, may be used to add an impetus to a new development programme. Such messages can add a personal touch

and concern for the welfare of a community and could help develop better attitudes towards new ideas. In this connection, a tape message from the chief minister of Maharashtra could be played back. He appeals to the farmers of Maharashtra to help solve unemployment problem in the country.

2) The tape recorder may be used in connection with broadcasts. For example, broadcasting of educational information may not be at times convenient for the rural listeners. These recordings or selections from recordings can then be used during the course of a training session. For example, recording of a radio programme in connection with family planning can be used at any time during a training programme.

3) In some communities, drama as a means of expression and entertainment carries a high rating. Dramatic interludes and conversation pieces can be used to pose problems and stimulate discussion that would lead to a group suggesting and seeking solutions to their own problems. Short dramatic interludes could be recorded and used by the trainers and extension workers. For example, a taped dramatic conversation regarding an irrigation problem in village can be played back in other villages by the extension worker to invite suggestions from the farmers and find out solutions.

4) In some training situations, it may be of value if the experiences recorded from members of one training courses are played back to another group of prospective trainees. In this way, an exchange of ideas might take place between those groups with similar problems. For example, views expressed by a farmer at the concluding session of a poultry training course can be taped and used in the next training course for improvement of the training programme.

5) Commentaries to accompany the use of filmstrips, or slides may be prerecorded. It must be understood that when this method is employed, the presentation loses its flexibility as it is no longer under the direct control of the instructor. But there is an advantage of having a carefully worded commentary. The accuracy and freshness of the presentation is thereby assured. It may be useful to know that many automatic slide projectors facilitate the automatic changing of slides at the appropriate places in the commentary.

6) For the training of groups in extension teaching methods

and procedures at meetings, an abbreviated recording of a typical meeting could be made and played over to the group to demonstrate specific points. Correct and incorrect methods may be shown.

Camera

It has been known for thousands of years that many substances are altered by exposure to sunlight. The skin, for example goes brown in the summer except where it is protected from the sun. It took many days to print the image with the help of light. The Greek word for light is 'photo' and for drawing is 'grapher'. The pictures made by light are, therefore, called drawings or pictures by light. The instrument used for drawing such pictures is called a camera.

Modern photography depends on the following things:

1) A source of light.

2) A subject or scene which reflects part of this light from the scene.

3) A camera, which is a dark box and holds the film that is coated with light sensitive emulsion.

4) A lens which when uncovered, redirects the rays from the subject to the lens.

5) Light sensitive film to record these light rays.

6) Chemicals, to develop and print it.

7) Printing paper and chemicals to turn the film negative into positive.

8) A light to expose the printing paper.

Mostly two types of cameras are used by extension workers to draw pictures. The first type is a box camera. It is a light tight box with lens at the one end to admit light and a place for a sensitive film at the other. There is a shutter in front of the lens or directly behind it to keep the light out except when picture is being taken. The second type of camera is the folding camera. These cameras differ from the box camera only in that they can be folded for ease in carrying. Some of them have no additional arrangements. Others provide a wide range of lens and shutter adjustments, require focussing and are equipped with many refinements.

Make Pictures Tell a Story

A good picture tells its own story so clearly that words are needed merely to fill in the details of names and places.

Pre-planning

Good story-telling photographs are not difficult to make, but they do require a little care on the part of the photographer before the shutter is snapped. Above all, there is need to study the scene you plan to photograph so that you can pick out the important things and eliminate the non-essentials. Keep the picture as simple as possible. This is not merely because simple things are easily understood; it is because the simpler a thing is, the more 'punch' one can get into the story.

Story Angle

How to make a picture tell a story? For example, suppose the picture story you want to tell is about the morning dash for the school bus. Obviously, you have to have a subject. This can be a friend or a young sister or brother. Then you need to have something which describes him as being on his way to school so he carries a book or two. Then you have to show, somehow, that he's on his way to the bus. Perhaps you try to include the school bus in the picture. Possibly you could make the shot from a position which gives you a part of the bus in the fore-ground with your subject running towards it.

This sort of thing needs just a little of planning. But what the planning amounts to is actually the simple business of asking yourself 'what do I have, to have to get the idea across?'

Sequence Picture

Another way to make pictures tell a story is to use two or more pictures in a sequence. In this case, the off-to-school story might begin with a photograph, showing the hero gulping down the last of his breakfast while mother, in the background, points to the clock. The second photograph would show him with his book, coming out of the house. And the final one would bring him in triumph to the door of the bus itself.

How to Take Pictures in Available Light

Perhaps the greatest advancement in the photographic field

has been the perfecting of available light photography for the amateur photographer. Because of continuing research, it is now possible to take pictures, indoors or outdoors, relying only on the existing light. The secret is in the film.

Extra-fast Film

The new extra-fast panchromatic film has a wider exposure latitude than ever before. It reaches deeper into shadows and records objects clearer whether the day is sunny or cloudy, whether the picture is taken indoors or outdoors. This is Kodak's new 'Verichrome' Pan film.

Use a Reflector

It is necessary to keep in mind certain points so as to get the best results under natural light situations.

When taking a photograph indoors, place the subject so that he faces the source of light, a door or window. It is important to remember that one side of the subject will necessarily be in shadow. In some picture-taking situations this sharp contrast between light and dark in a subject is desirable. But photographers who desire even lighting may use a reflector.

Any bedsheet, white cardboard or even a sheet of newspaper will serve as a reflector. By placing and aiming the reflector properly one can bounce existing light into shadowed areas. Reflectors should be placed high or low depending on the camera and aimed at the subject in such a way that they catch the light and bounce it where the photographer wants it.

Avoid Glare

Be alert to see that none of the room lights produce a glare on the camera lens. This can ruin a good indoor natural light shot.

Outdoors

Outdoors natural light photography has many advantages. People generally frown or squint when photographed in bright sunlight, but are more relaxed and at ease if snapped in shade. Also during the rainy season Kodak's new 'Verichrome' Pan film allows interesting, natural-looking pictures to be taken on cloudy days.

Pictures are Where One Finds Them

With a clear sky overhead and bright sunshine all round, our country, rightly called the 'land of sunshine and colours' is full of opportunity for outdoor photography. From the snowclad peaks of the north to the lush greenness of the south, a halt anywhere in the countryside can yield a charming picture, sparkling with a beauty of its own.

In landscape pictures, though, a forceful foreground interest is of enormous importance. A human figure, or some other dominating mass in the foreground, not only improves the composition but effectively lends depth to the scene. Often, too, it adds a 'story-telling' element to the picture.

There is slight difficulty in keeping the whole picture in focus. It sometimes works to focus on the foreground figures only, and leave the background to take care of itself. It is better to set the lens at about 15 feet and stop down to f/16. When your foreground subject is 15 feet or further from the camera the whole picture will be as sharp as one could reasonably wish. This, of course, is the principle on which a box camera works.

Indeed, a box camera is perfectly capable of producing fine outdoor pictures, when the man behind the camera has an eye for choosing the right subject. The main difficulty usually lies in imagining what the scene will look like when it is reduced to the size of print, and rendered in black-and-white. The photographer's skill comes in selecting the right combination of highlights and shadows, and in studying his view-finder carefully to judge the relative size of objects in the finished picture.

Another important part of an outdoor picture is a well-balanced background. Fortunately nature's own backdrop, the sky, is nearly always ideal, a middle-toned sky, dotted perhaps with small wandering clouds, lends a rich romantic charm to almost any picture.

Pictures are everywhere. If one has an eye for composition, and reasonable knowledge of how the camera works—there is hardly a minute of the day in which you cannot make a fine picture.

Background to Characters

In a character portrait (indeed any portrait) its background should be so meticulously planned as to be appropriate with the models. Careful subduing of these may require to 'play up' the model. A tonal background is much easier to handle, while at the same time infinite variations with these tones may be attempted and achieved.

In any case, incongruous and obtrusive objects in the background are to be avoided.

Use Imagination

Next to a camera and film the most important ingredient for picture-taking is a good imagination. Without imagination, a picture is just a flat statement of fact, which might be likened to a teller of jokes who relates a story without expression and then kills the punch line.

It is imagination that sets one photographer apart from others. There are plenty of excellent technicians among the photographers, men who know how to make perfectly exposed negatives and excellent prints. But if the photographer has both these qualities and imagination—he's on his way to success.

In photographing a building, for instance, some people will use a head-on approach. The better photographer will try to tell a story. Perhaps he will photograph it through a pattern of old iron grill-work making the picture say, "Here is a modern structure that contrasts with the older type of architecture. See the contrast between the curlicues of the old iron work and the clean lines of the modern building." One picture is a 'map' of the subject, the other says something that the photographer thought and believed in when he took the picture.

When picturing a landscape, one photographer will step out of the car, set his camera and shoot from where he is at that moment. Another will take the trouble to scout around before clicking the shutter. Perhaps he will find a curving tree branch that frames a beautiful view, or he will place someone in the foreground with his or her back to the camera looking outward to the view he is going to photograph. In this way he will transform his picture from a straight shot of the countryside into something artistic.

When taking a close-up of a person, some photographers stand the subject in bright sunlight in front of a house wall and click the shutter. The better photographer puts his subject in the more comfortable shade, or at least turns the face away from the strong sunlight and poses the subject doing something interesting.

Imagination will put new glitter on old things and will lead to seek new and better viewpoints. Get in and look out, go up and look down, you will find interesting pictures, subjects that you never saw before.

RELATIVE EFFECTIVENESS OF METHODS

Two factors are considered in evaluating the relative effectiveness of the teaching methods or channels of communication. Firstly, the success of the method in influencing people to make the desired changes. Secondly, the amount of the teaching effort expended on it.

The total influence of a particular means of teaching may be great because of emphasis placed on it in the extension teaching plan. For example, the tremendous influence of the method demonstration meeting in agricultural extension work as is evident by its extensive use by the extension worker. On the other hand the total influence of a method may be relatively small owing to little use of it in extension teaching. This explains the relatively small influence of farm visits in changing the agricultural practices.

A unit of time devoted to a particular method of teaching may yield much larger returns than a corresponding amount of effort expended on some other method of teaching. The news story, the radio and circular letter are examples of large returns per unit on the time devoted to these means of teaching by extension workers. The exhibition and result demonstration are examples that influence comparatively few people per unit of extension worker's time.

As discussed earlier it is advisable to use a combination of teaching methods. The combined effectiveness of two or more methods used to complement each other may be greater than the sum of the effectiveness of the same methods when employed independently. The most successful extension worker utilises from the entire teaching effort the best combination of the teaching methods available to him in such a manner as to ensure the possible target accomplishment. However, determining the influence and cost of each method used, is difficult to measure duc to the informal nature of extension work and the numerous opportunities for learning available to rural people.

CHAPTER 5

Extension Programme Planning

The educational efforts of any organisation should be to teach persons how to think and not what to think. It is the function of the educational system to teach people to determine accurately their own needs and the solution of their problems, to help them acquire knowledge and to inspire them to action. But it should be clearly understood that the action must be their own and made of their own knowledge and convictions. The ultimate objective of extension teaching is to promote the physical, mental, spiritual and social growth of the individual farmer, his wife and children. This can be done by helping them in analysing their own problems, in finding solutions to them, and in bringing about active participation in formulating and carrying out the plans necessary to put these solutions into effect. One should not act on the assumption that any group of persons will act on the plan about which they have not been consulted. In order to obtain their participation, it is necessary that they should be involved in the preparation of the plan.

PROGRAMME PLANNING PROCESS

Programme planning is a continuous series of activities or operations leading to the development of a definite plan of action to accomplish particular objectives. It is the process by which people work together to determine goals. In this process they agree and feel that the goals and experiences may help them in reaching their objectives. The extension programme planning process is presented in figure 5.1. The process has eight steps which are described in detail in the

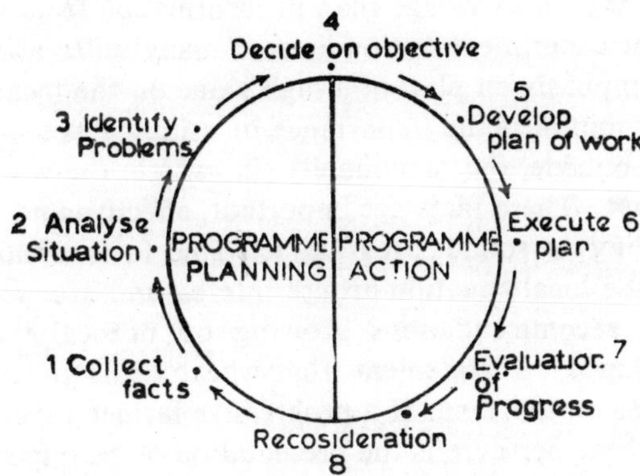

Fig. 5.1 Extension Programme Planning Process.

following pages.

The first four steps are included under programme planning while the remaining four steps are grouped under programme action. As stated earlier the programme planning process is a continuous one and it is better if it starts from the first step and moves to the last step. Each step has its own importance and if any one step is missed the programme may not be realistic, and naturally there will not be the expected change or development due to that programme. It is, therefore, necessary that steps of the programme planning process should not be overlooked or missed while preparing and implementing the programme.

1) Collect Facts

Facts are the foundation stones upon which the community leaders and the problem committee build and carry out their programmes. It is the responsibility of the change agent (extension worker) to assemble and interpret factual information for the use of the community leaders.

The local situation is the bench mark from where people should start the process of programme planning. People are more concerned with facts that grow out of or are related to their own experiences. For instance, people are generally more interested in facts secured from a result demonstration held in their own village than in information from a demonstration or experiment station located many miles away.

The emphasis on placing a high value on the local situation does not minimise the importance of using facts secured from sources outside the community in which the work is being carried out. These facts are important, effective and assist in determining a sound programme. The facts obtained from outside the local situation arouse interest and are valuable in deciding recommendations growing out of local experiences. For instance, a statement that wheat yields under irrigated conditions on the farm of a progressive farmer gave 15 quintals of wheat per acre is the presentation of an important fact about a local situation. If this statement is followed by the report of 75 national demonstration results stating an average of 12 quintals of wheat per acre, then the local fact just presented is more nearly clinched. If the agricultural university experiment station data shows the same results, it is very likely that the village planning committee will consider this fact seriously while planning the wheat programme.

The assembling of the facts pertaining to local situations is a continuous activity. It is important that facts about local situations be regularly recorded in the project file by the change agent. It will be convenient to maintain the record of facts each day in a daily diary. Afterwards this information may be transferred to the permanent project file for later reference. Facts may be secured from revenue records, panchayat samiti records, local newspapers or magazines, by personal visits, records of demonstrations, surveys, reports from key leaders, conferences and meetings and other sources.

2) Analyse Situation

After assembling the facts pertaining to local situations it is important to analyse these facts in such a way that they will be useful to individuals or committees. This analysis or interpretation means a translation of these facts into familiar language or terms. It also means an explanation of the meaning of facts as they apply to the local farm or community. Interpretation of facts involves careful reasoning backed up by experience and judgement. The change agents sometimes with the help of specialists or technicians and a committee of experienced farmers, are in the best position to interpret information in terms of local adaptation.

3) Identify Problems

Facts about local situations after analysis are helpful in identifying the problems. When facts are properly interpreted they help the change agents and leaders in showing the situation as it is. The facts arouse the interest of the people. They identify the problems and needs and indicate solutions to problems. They also point out weaknesses, indicate shortages and direct attention to undesirable trends. In order to have adequate facts about a local situation it is generally necessary and often advisable to secure information that falls within three categories, namely:

i) Trends (local trends compared with state and national trends).
ii) The present local situation.
iii) Recommendations.

These three types of information can be illustrated by relating them to the facts that should be assembled about a particular local situation. Wheat cultivation is used as an example in the following lines:

i) Trend information on local wheat cultivation.
a) Changes in the wheat area for the past 10 years.
b) Changes in wheat yields per acre for the past 10 years.
c) Changes in wheat fertilisation/irrigation/cultivation for the past 10 years.
d) Changes in wheat varieties.
e) Changes in marketing systems.
f) Changes in the quality of wheat produced.
g) Other changes.

ii) Information on present wheat cultivation.
a) Area under wheat in the locality.
b) Wheat production per acre.
c) Level of fertiliser use per acre for wheat.
d) Method of irrigation adopted.
e) Systems of marketing wheat.
f) Others which may help to identify problems and obstacles to wheat cultivation.

iii) Recommendations.

The change agent after consulting the specialists and the experienced farmers should arrive at certain recommendations for increasing the wheat yields. These recommendations may be in terms of a package of practices for wheat cultivation of that area as a short-term measure. It may also be a long-term recommendation like developing the irrigation potential of the area.

4) Decide on Objectives

Objectives are expressions of the ends towards which efforts are directed. The objective has a definite meaning. One has to know that a great deal of thought and planning has to be put into efforts to reach the objective. The success or failure of a particular movement is judged in terms of whether or not the objective is reached. The success in reaching one objective affects other tasks and has an accumulated effect on the outcome of the project. For instance, if an individual farmer decides his objective as raising 10 quintals of wheat per acre and if he cannot succeed then it has an effect on the total wheat production of the area and finally on the national income. If large numbers of farmers do not reach the desired objective of raising the wheat then it has an accumulated effect on the wheat yield of the area. In other words, objective is that which a person, group or agency sets before itself as an object or condition to be attained. There is a slight distinction between objectives and goals. Objectives are the directions of movement, while a goal is the distance in any given direction one expects to go during a given period of time. Objective, aim and purpose are used synonymously by educators, but generally only one word, i.e., 'objective' is used for these terms.

Objectives can be grouped into three levels depending on their specificity.

1) Fundamental objectives are the all-inclusive objectives set for society. These objectives are found in the constitution of the country. The fundamental rights of citizens, good life, better citizenship, democracy and the development of the individual are a few examples of these objectives.

2) General. objectives are more definite than fundamental

objectives. They are generally found in the statements of policies and purposes of the organisation. Providing better recreational and housing facilities to the rural people is an example of this objective.

3) Working objectives are the specific items which are to be achieved. These may be stated from the change agent's standpoint and from the standpoint of the people. It is important to harmonise what rural people feel, what they need and what professional extension workers think they ought to have. In an ideal situation there would be perfect agreement between these two. For example, to increase the wheat yield per acre by using improved varieties, following the *sara* method of irrigation, etc.

While stating the objectives it is necessary to test them for their usefulness in meeting the standards of educational attainments and for achieving the desired targets.

a) The objectives should be clearly stated. They should identify the people concerned or to be concerned, the changes the people desire to make and the content or subject matter areas involved.

b) The objectives should be achievable considering the people concerned and the available resources.

c) The objectives should be developmental and lead to an expansion of interest and satisfactions.

d) The objectives should be such that they can be evaluated and evidences of accomplishments can be identified.

5) Develop Plan of Work

Plan of work is a definite outline of procedure for solving the different problems of the extension programme. Such a plan identifies specifically the different jobs that need to be done, the means to be used, the methods of using them and when each specific phase or part of the plan is to be executed in order to achieve the objectives. The plan of work should be a written statement of detailed action. It should guide teaching in different phases of the programme. It is a blueprint for the extension workers and the people to follow in moving forward on their programme. The plan of work is usually chalked out for a year and therefore, it is called as annual plan of work. The extension staff, lay leaders and appropriate subject matter specialists should be involved in development of the plan of work.

The major decisions involved in developing a plan of work are indicated here:

a) Decide WHAT different things or jobs need to be done to accomplish the objectives. This will include such things as attitudes or interests that need to be developed, goals or purposes that need to be established and understanding and abilities that need to be developed. These job requirements are required to be planned and executed in such a way that those participating will have motivated educational experience.

b) Decide HOW best do each of the specific jobs that need be done in order to accomplish the objectives. This will involve making decisions on questions like, what type of learning experience needs to be provided and what teaching tools, devices and techniques need to be employed to do each of these jobs, etc.

c) Decide WHO will be responsible for planning, preparing and executing each of the specific learning experiences and plans or jobs that need to be done. This will involve such decisions as what other group, agencies or organisations will be cooperating. Will a specialist be used and for what specific job?, etc.

d) Decide WHEN each specific phase or part of the plan including meetings to be held, news stories to be written, radio-broadcasts to be made, tours, demonstrations, etc., will be executed or carried to completion. This will involve developing a detailed and complete calendar for the programme to be carried out relative to each of the overall problems of the extension programme. This calendar of work (activities and events) will include the chronological listing of scheduled major events and activities of importance to be undertaken by the extension staff during a given year and is included in the annual plan of work.

6) Execute Plan

Executing the plan means carrying through the previously planned educational jobs and learning situations as set forth in the plan of work and the teaching plans. This assumes that a programme is planned, and a plan of work is developed. This forms the base for programme execution.

The programme execution should be coordinated within the extension service and other agencies and organisations as set forth in the plan of work. Secondly, the calendar of activities and events should be followed as planned. A variety of appropriate techniques, methods and materials should be used as planned. The subject matter should be appropriate to the objective to be achieved and the people involved and used as planned in the teaching plan. Adequate and appropriate training and other assistance as planned should be given to lay leaders in assuming their planned and accepted responsibilities in the execution of the programme. The plan for sharing of programme action responsibilities by the extension staff, other professional people and lay people should be followed.

The execution of plan should be carried out as decided and unnecessary changes should not be made. If adjustments are to be made then they should be made on the basis of reevaluation, replanning and decision, and they should be accepted by all concerned.

7) Evaluation of Progress

Evaluation is the process of determining the extent to which objectives have been attained. The programme accomplishments are the changes in people and the changes in their economic and social situations resulting from the programme. Information which reveals the extent to which objectives are reached is needed to evaluate accomplishments. This will help in determining how far an activity has progressed and how much further it should be carried to accomplish objectives. The amount of accomplishment judged to be satisfactory should be determined in the light of the potential for improvement in the area, the complexity of the problem. objectives and the resources available.

Importance

Evaluation is an essential step in the extension educational process. It is through the process of evaluation that one arrives at judgements or conclusions that will aid in decision making. To clarify this it will be useful to define several terms. A decision is a choice among alternatives. Judgement is an assignment of values to the alternatives. The evaluation from this point of view provides information for decision making. It will help in decisions regarding continuation, redirection, reemphasis of the present programme or decisions as to the need for new programmes. Thus evaluation is an important and integral part of all teaching and programme planning work.

a) Without appraisal of results there is no sound basis for improving the work.

b) It helps to identify needs for concentrated effort.

c) It gives assurance and confidence to the persons concerned.

d) It has a value in creating public confidence by presenting rational facts.

e) It will help in judging the value of methods or devices used.

f) It helps the extension teaching by compelling the extension workers to define the objectives clearly.

g) It will help in choosing the best tools in the teaching plan.

Thus, evaluation improves the professional attitudes of those who use scientific techniques.

In the previous sections, it was seen that the programme planning process requires collection of facts, fixing of programme objectives, preparation of plans of work and implementation of hese plans through appropriate action for achieving the esired results. Evaluation can and should take place in relation to each of these stages. At each stage the performance of those involved in the process can be measured against standards which have been fixed for it. One can ask, "How good is the planning organisation? Dó the ›bjectives correspond to the needs of the clientele? How adequate is the plan of work? How well are the plans followed? And what has actually been accomplished?"

The foregoing questions can be more precise. The effectiveness of evaluation in each case will depend on the pertinent questions asked and the nature of the responses. The questions mentioned here are widely applicable but they will require adaptation to specific standards or conditions which are to be met in each situation. The situation in an Indian village will be different from what it would be in a comparable situation, say in Indonesia. It is the responsibility of each agency or individual making use of these questions, to select the specific standards that will be appropriate and relevant to the situation involved. Another point to remember is the intent of the question and its appropriateness to local conditions.

Who Should Do the Evaluation?

After fixing the conditions and standards in relation to each stage, one is confronted with practical questions such as who should carry out the evaluation. When should it be done? What information will be required? And how does one go about collecting this information? The following are a few suggestions in answer to these questions.

In most of the cases the agency undertakes its own evaluation. This self evaluation is useful from time to time, to supplement the evaluation made by competent persons or groups outside the agency for overcoming biases and for introducing new ideas. Self evaluation may be done through a committee or some individual assigned to do this job. It can be done by those who are directly responsible for the phase concerned. In such cases provision should be made for coordination to ensure that evaluations are in line with the overall purposes of the agency.

When Should Evaluation be Done?

The evaluation of all the stages could be done at one time, that is, at the end of a programme year. In some instances it will be better to evaluate each stage as it develops in the total planning process. One need not wait for the final results of the programme in order to evaluate its objectives. In fact, these early evaluations may lead to adjustments which will contribute appreciably to the effectiveness with which results can be accomplished. Whether evaluation is made out at the end of a programme or is carried out as a continuous process, provision for it ought to be included in the planning and implementation procedures adopted by the agency.

From Whom Should Information be Collected?

The information required for evaluation can be taken from the various prepared documents such as written plans, records, reports, etc. It will help, if these are prepared in such a way as to facilitate the collection of the information useful for evaluation. Information can be collected from the people directly concerned with the programme. Information from these extension staff, committee members and local leaders may be obtained verbally or in writing.

In some instances, it may be necessary to use broad survey techniques for collecting the desired information in evaluating the results of a programme. This information may be collected at three points of attainment.

1) Bench mark stage: It is the initial stage when the extension programme is to be introduced. This is the point from which the people start in their change of behaviour.

2) Interim stage: This is any stage in the progress of the people towards the objective.

3) Final stage: After the completion of the programme, evaluation would be undertaken to measure the attainment of the final objective. One has to find out if few, some or all the people have reached that objective. It helps in deciding the retention of the objective in the plan of work or substituting it with another one and deciding the effectiveness of the teaching methods.

The surveys can be done by personal interviews or by sending out questionnaires (mailed questionnaires) to the people concerned. It is more feasible to interview or get questionnaires filled in of a few people who are representative of the group as a whole.

How is Information to be Collected?

There are two methods, which are normally used in collecting information for evaluation. In the census method information from all the people or the population involved is collected. However, it may not always be possible to obtain information from all the population and hence appropriate sampling techniques are required to be used.

Sampling means selecting a small number from the whole concerned group, from which an estimate can then be made for the whole group. The use of sampling implies obtaining of information from a small number of carefully selected people whose answers will be typical of a larger number of people.

The sampling technique helps in saving time and money. It is helpful for detailed and accurate studies as the information from a few people is required to be collected.

Methods of Drawing the Sample

Several methods of drawing samples are used in evaluation work. A few of them are discussed here.

List sampling: There are two ways of drawing samples in list sampling. One method is to select a random group of people from any office or other complete numbered list. Random number tables are developed for this purpose and are normally given in statistical books. These numbers in the table are absolutely random and enable one to draw sample more or less mechanically. Random selection means that every person on the list has as much chance of being selected as another.

Another method is preparing and using alphabetical lists. Arrange the respondents or the population in alphabetical order. One starts with 'A's and 'n'th name is taken until you have as many as needed. If it is planned to have a 10 per cent sample from the total list then every tenth name is taken for inclusion in the sample.

Block or area sampling: This means that one takes a random sample of areas in which people live, instead of random sample of the individuals themselves. In this way, instead of the people probably being scattered all over the country (or state), they will be grouped together so that an interviewer can carry out several interviews in one section with very little distance between interviews.

Stratified sampling: The methods just described illustrate methods which do not aim at bringing into the sample certain proportion of people with certain characteristics. These methods are on the basis of random selection in which the selected sample is in the same proportion that they are represented in the whole population. In the stratified sampling method the population is categorised in different classes and a sample is drawn from these classes. If one knows the degree of certain classes of people being represented in the population, then on the basis of this knowledge attempt is made to get that definite proportion of certain characteristics in the sample.

Quota sampling: Quota sampling is a refined variation of

stratified sampling. In quota sampling an attempt is made to include in the sample some of every known kind of individual in the population. If possible, the same proportion of each is included in the sample as exists in the population.

Purposive sampling or judgement sampling: The sampling methods just described above depend on objective procedures which should result in representative samples. In these methods everyone in the population has an equal chance of being selected. There are samples which are chosen on the basis of the judgement of the selector. This is also called purposive sampling, where the sampler handpicks each individual for inclusion in the sample, making up what is intended to be a sample representative of the population from which it is chosen.

The idea in judgement sampling is to make the sample as representative as possible, so that measurements or observations on it can be taken as virtually equivalent to similar measurements on the whole population. This should be in the mind of the sampler while taking the sample and this will influence his selection as this freedom of choice is not given to him in random sampling. Most samplers, while selecting a representative sample, will deliberately reject abnormal cases or if they feel that the sample should be representative of the abnormal as well as the normal then he will deliberately balance the different categories accordingly.

However, there is a feeling that the sampler's claims to be able to select a representative sample by personal judgement are largely unfounded, and that his selection is subject to all sorts of biases, psychological and physical. To avoid these biases and to provide an estimate of the representativeness of the sample it is better to adopt more vigorous methods of selecting the sample. These methods have already been described earlier.

Measuring devices: Most of the extension programmes are educational in nature. In addition to the physical achievements in the programme, importance is attached to the attainment of the educational objectives. Some of the devices used for measuring the progress towards the educational objective are given here.

a) *Value scales* are used to determine the value people place on things and to show what people think is important, e.g., religious value, economic value, scientific value, etc.

b) *Attitude scales* show how people feel towards things. These may be for or against feelings towards certain problems e.g., child marriage, family planning, etc.

c) *Opinion polls* are held to know the opinions of people on certain issues. It may be in simple 'yes' or 'no' form or free answer questions, e.g., surveys to know the voting behaviour of the people in election.

d) *Knowledge and comprehension tests* are used for finding out whether a person understands or can apply certain acquired knowledge in a given situation, e.g., knowledge about paddy cultivation.

e) *Interest checks* are used to find out the interests of the people in different activities or programmes, e.g., interest in family planning programme.

f) *Skill or performance rating* are used to determine the amount of skill attainment by the people, e.g., skill in driving a tractor.

g) *Adoption of practices* is for finding out the extent to which the improved practices are being used by the people, e.g., studying the adoption of practices in wheat.

h) *Case history* technique is used for studying in detail one unit of the population, e.g., case study of a progressive farmer or a youth club.

The devices stated here are used in collecting information for evaluation. In these devices most of the information is asked through questions. The mechanical construction and the appearance of the questionnaire are important. The questions should be short, clear and concise and placed in logical order. Ample space should be provided for all written answers.

After collecting the data it is necessary to summarise it to give a picture of the project. The data may be tabulated and interpreted properly. It should be prepared in the form of a written report for the use of all concerned. It should be remembered that data should never be collected or presented for just its own sake. Data is collected to answer a question in your mind and hence when the data is interpreted it should give you an answer to that question. The report should be a summary of those answers.

8) Reconsideration

The findings of evaluation need to be used by applying it to future work. A report of the findings or information obtained in evaluation is purely a tool and not an objective. A report is written for clarifying the thinking of the evaluator and for presenting it to other persons. When a teacher takes a test in the class, he finds that he failed to teach certain topics in the class prior to the test. In this case the teacher need not write a report of what the test has shown, but has to reconsider the findings and apply them to a future situation. The teacher should try to make up his failure in the days ahead while teaching the course the next time. Secondly, he should try to present those ideas that he failed to present well in a different way to see if they are properly understood by the students.

The important thing is that the evaluation process has not served its purpose unless the conclusion drawn from it has entered the continuing plans of the workers. In other words it is the reconsideration of the whole issue in the light of the findings of the evaluation. If it is found that the present activities of the worker fail in reaching certain objectives or certain defined people then the worker has not improved himself professionally. The value of his work will be poor and he will have to attempt to modify his activities so that they might or will reach the objectives or the people. Thus the findings of evaluation need to be presented either by talk with the local leader or in the form of a report for reconsideration. The way in which findings are presented for reconsideration is determined by the audience or the reader. If they lack the training or background for interpreting the statistical table or discussions but are supposed to use the findings in their work, the findings should be entirely interpreted for them and presented to them in terms of activities or recommendations that they can understand. If the purpose of the presentation is to provide statistical proof for a decision or recommendation, the statistics need to be included in the presentation or publication. If the audience or readers are interested in the procedure involved in collecting the data, that should be included. If the inclusion of such details detracts from the importance of the findings or confuses certain types of audience or readers, it should be limited to the barest essentials. In many cases, the findings from surveys have to be presented in more than one way to meet the needs of several kinds of audiences or readers.

IMPORTANCE OF EXTENSION PROGRAMME

The extension programmes are useful for the following reasons.

1) To ensure careful consideration of what is to be done and why.

2) To furnish a guide against which new proposals are to be judged.

3) To present in written form a statement for public use.

4) To establish objectives with which progress can be measured and evaluated.

5) To have a means of choosing the important from the incidental problems and the permanent from the temporary changes.

6) To present mistaking the means for the end and to develop both felt and unfelt needs.

7) To give continuity during changes of personnel.

8) To aid in the development of leadership.

9) To avoid waste of time and money and promote general efficiency.

10) To coordinate the efforts of the different people working for rural development.

CHARACTERISTICS OF A GOOD PROGRAMME

An extension programme is a carefully prepared statement written in a form that clearly sets forth the significant changes that are needed in the behaviour of the people and in the conditions in which they live, to be attained over a period of time. A good programme should have the following characteristics.

1) The written programme should be suitable for use by the staff, planning groups, and other individuals or groups concerned with the programme.

2) It should state the primary facts that clearly reveal the situation on major subjects or problem areas.

3) It should clearly state the important problems or needs identified by the staff and the people in the programming

process.

4) It should state both long-term and short-term objectives for each major subject or problem that is to be focussed on in programme execution over a period of time.

5) It should state the objectives of the programme clearly and meaningfully.

6) It should specify the subject matter related to each objective that is highly significant to people, socially and economically.

7) It should include the summary of the long-term programme prepared in a form suitable for public distribution.

8) It should be made available in a summary form to all members of the planning groups and the professional staff.

9) It should be circulated by appropriate means so that the general public can understand its nature and objectives.

10) It should be used as a basis for developing an annual plan for work.

PARTICIPATION OF ORGANISATIONS IN PROGRAMME PLANNING

The programme development process includes many actions. To accomplish the objectives it is necessary to have some form of organisation of the people of the area. The composition and structure of such organisation is dependent on the relevant social systems, interests and nature of the geographic areas. It is necessary to see that in these organisations participation of the people, local leaders, voluntary agencies and institutions is actively sought.

This council or committee responsible for programme planning and implementation should be given adequate amount of time to work with the extension staff to ensure success. There should be proper coordination between these voluntary agencies and the extension organisation at the grass-root level. The field of rural development is vast and the need for involvement of the people and their organisations is great. The number of agencies working for rural development are few and therefore, every one sincerely engaged in the task is welcome. Only the effort has to be coordinated, so that it produces good results.

There are 5000 blocks in India. Each block has a block

panchayat samiti consisting of peoples' representatives linked with local panchayats elected by the people. They are supported in the planning process by the block development officer, subject matter extension officers, village development officers and other local functionaries.

The spread of the voluntary agencies is not eyen in all these blocks. There are thousands of blocks without any voluntary agency worth the name functioning in the field of rural development. The agencies which are in existence may cover wider areas, e.g. khadi and village industries. Some of them may take up work in smaller areas comprising a block or two while a few of them may take up a village or only a few villages. The number of voluntary agencies in the last category appear to be largest.

The extension organisation has the availability of technical knowledge, guidance, implements and equipment, and financial resources. Voluntary agencies are characterised by greater commitment to people, greater intensity of work, greater continuity and greater acceptability among the community. When the two work in coordination it is in the interest of the people. This will help in utilising the capacity of the voluntary agency working in a chosen area with the technical and financial support from the extension organisation. The voluntary agencies may be encouraged to expand their area of operation and fields of activity if the performance of the voluntary agency is good. In other words, the extension organisation's objective so far as the participation of the voluntary agency is concerned should be to help it grow to its fullest potential and for that purpose to place all reasonable resources at its disposal.

For better participation of these agencies a provision will have to be made to nominate chief executives of the voluntary organisations to the block panchayat samiti and/or zilla parishad depending upon the size and extent of their operations. This is necessary both to ensure the organisations' accountability to the larger community, and to put development in the chosen area and the chosen fields in the perspective of the total development of the block or the district.

Involvement of People in Programme Planning

All people whose welfare is affected by the programme may

be involved in this process. Local people with leadership abilities may be requested to serve on the formal committees responsible for programme planning. Secondly, local people who have special and vital interest in success in a specific subject matter area such as cotton cultivation, cattle, recreation, etc., may also be involved. Thirdly, the people with special talents or resource people such as specialised extension personnel, production and marketing specialists, entomologists, representatives of credit agencies and many others who have something to contribute need to be involved in this process.

The purpose of involving people is that the programmes are meant for the people and hence it is better if the plans are prepared by the people who are to be benefited by that programme. It will help the people in fulfilling their responsibilities as citizens in a political democracy by preserving and strengthening values like freedom, progress and success.

Programme planning is an excellent means of developing the leadership qualities of the people. Effective organisation. systematic fact collection, vigorous analysis and skilful decision making are all important parts of successful programme planning. Developing skills in these operations lead to the development of competent leadership.

Engaging in programme planning has proved to be an invaluable educational experience for all those who actively engage in the process. Thus the experiences gained by the people who participate in these planning sessions contribute much to their knowledge of facts and to their skill in making wise choices.

The participation of the people in the programme planning process normally gives them a proprietary interest in seeing that an action programme is carried out. If they have taken enough interest to study very carefully the various aspects of a given subject matter area, they would probably develop enough interest to see that it leads to action.

SURVEYS

In programme planning facts form an important base. These facts can be collected by conducting surveys. The survey is a method of analysis in scientific and orderly form for defined purpose of a given situation or problem or population.

Types of Surveys

Surveys can be classified into various types according to their subject matter, technique of data collection, regularity and such other factors.

There are different subject areas in which detailed information is required for various purposes. These surveys are conducted for collecting this information.

1) Demographic Surveys: This includes surveys about organizations and their working. Information regarding family or household composition, marital status, fertility, age etc. is collected through these surveys.

2) Social environment Surveys: These surveys cover social and economic factors to which people are subjected. It mainly include occupation, income, housing conditions and social amenities.

3) Social activities Surveys: In these surveys human behavioural data is collected. This data relates with different events, actions or behaviour of individuals in the society.

4) Opinion and attitude Surveys: In these surveys data regarding the level of information, opinions and attitudes of people towards various social factors, their motives and expectations is collected.

Besides the above classes the other types may be combination of various types namely, socio-economic, socio-political or socio-psychological surveys.

The survey can also be classified according to the techniques used in data collection.

1) General or specific surveys: General surveys are conducted for collecting general information like population, institutions or phenomena without any particular object. Census of population every tenth year is a typical example of such a survey. The specific surveys like adoption behaviour of farmers are conducted for specific purpose or for testing validity of some theory.

2) Regular or ad-hoc Surveys: Regular surveys are held after regular intervals to study the trend or the effect of time on the phenomena under study. Family budget survey, Rural credit survey are the examples of these surveys. Ad-voc surveys are undertaken

once for all. They are mostly undertaken for testing the hypothesis or supplementing some missing information regarding any research problems.

3) Preliminary or final Surveys: A preliminary survey is held for obtaining firsthand knowledge of the universe to be surveyed. It helps in getting acquainted with the problem and the nature of respondents from whom the information is to be collected for final survey. After collecting the information from preliminary survey the final survey is conducted for collecting detailed information.

4) Census or Sample Surveys: In the census surveys information from all the people or population involved is collected, Information from every single unit in the universe is collected, sampling surveys are conducted by selecting a small number of sample from the whole concerned group and collecting information from this group. Sample surveys are becoming popular due to their convenience in collecting information by saving time and cost. The collected data (information) obtained through proper survey method is tabulated and analysed. The conclusions and generalizations are drawn on the basis of the collected data and are put up in the form of a report. In addition to the above the surveyor is expected to offer his opinion and suggestions regarding the problem under study.

CHAPTER 6

Extension Administration

In extension administration two things are important. The first is the knowledge of administration, that can be developed by administrators. This knowledge must be reinforced with an understanding of many local, statewide and national factors that affect its application. Such knowledge will make the administrators aware of some of the unanticipated consequences of their decisions. Secondly, the skill and the knowledge possessed by the administrators should be used by them in solving the problems of the organisation of which they are members. Unless this is brought in practice it will have no utility for the organisation.

Meaning

Administration can be defined as the guidance, leadership and control of the efforts of a group of individuals towards some common goal. According to this definition the essence of administration is the ability of the administrator to plan large projects, weld together an organisation for its accomplishment, keep the organisation functioning smoothly and efficiently and achieve the agreed upon objectives well within the allotment of the personnel, time and resources available, and without doing all the work himself.

Scope

The scope of administration can be expressed in terms of the functional elements indicated by the letters of the word POSDCORB. This word is made up of initials and indicates the following activities.

P — stands for *planning*, i.e., working out in broad outline the things to be done and the methods to be adopted for accomplishing the purpose in hand.

O — stands for *organisation*, i.e., building up the structure of authority through which the entire work to be done is arranged into well defined sub-divisions and coordination.

S — stands for *staffing*, i.e., appointing suitable persons to the various posts under the organisation and the whole of personnel management.

D — stands for *directing*, i.e., making decisions, issuing orders and instructions for the guidance of the staff.

CO — stands for *coordination*, i.e., interrelating various parts of the work and eliminating overlapping and conflict.

R — stands for *reporting*, i.e., keeping both the superiors and subordinates informed of what is going on, and arranging for the collection of such information through inspection, research and records.

B — stands for *budgeting*, which is more concerned with the financial affairs of the organisation.

These POSDCORB activities are common to all fields of administration and therefore, are also applicable to the extension administration.

Basic Principles of Administration

It is assumed that increased effectiveness of administration will occur when the principles of administration are followed. These principles are also called guidelines as they guide the administrators in the performance of their job.

1) *Principle of Hierarchy*

The members of the organisation are arranged in a definite subordinate—superordinate hierarchy of line positions (e.g., classes I, II, III and IV). It is also known as the 'scaler process', wherein lines of positional authority and responsibility run upward and downward through several levels with a broad base at the bottom and a single head at the top in order to preserve the 'unity of command'.

In the effective organisation each worker knows who is his supervisor and each supervisor knows whom he is expected to supervise. If a worker is subject to orders from several supervisors (as in the case of village development officer), he gets confused, inefficient and irresponsible. In this arrangement the authority of making vital decisions is entrusted with a specialised person located at the helm of the organisation.

2) *Principle of Authority*

Effective administration will occur when the authority allocated to an individual or group of individuals is sufficient. The authority and the responsibility should be clearly defined and understood by all persons in the organisation. The different types of authorities are given in the following pages.

3) *Principle of Responsibility with Matching Authority*

The individual should not be burdened only with responsibilities but should also be provided with matching authority. This is more important in a decentralised form of administration. Responsibility without authority is just like leaving an individual to fight with a tiger without a gun or weapon.

4) *Principle of Span of Control*

Span of control is the number of subordinates one has to supervise. In general, the span of control is such as to permit as much decentralisation of decision-making as is needed. It helps in attaining quality decisions. It results in increased effectiveness and efficiency in attaining the organisational objectives. Some of the factors influencing the span of control include (a) the intensity and frequency of the need to see the chief, (b) the magnitude of their problems, (c) the age of the agency, (d) the professional competence and length of service of the staff, (e) the size of the agency, (f) the size of the geographic area in which the supervisor must operate, (g) the importance of the decisions which the supervisor must make, (h) the degree of control that must be exercised, and (i) the degree of repetitiveness of the work to be done.

5) *Principle of Communication*

There should be a two-way channel of communication, both vertical and horizontal in the organisation. Communication ensures common understanding of organisational values and objectives. Clear and proper assignments of authority and functions are required for success in large operations. Employees want to know what is going on. Without a broad sharing of information and purpose, their morale will be low and the agency's task will be more difficult.

6) *Principle of Organisational Structure*

The organisation can no longer remain fixed or static. Changes in basic objectives, in size of staff, in professional competency, adjustments in programme emphasis, in the nature of institutional relationships within which the organisation must operate will have to be made. Similarly the need for long range as well as short range planning of programmes, personnel and finances may require many adjustments in the form of the administrative organisational structure. In short the organisational structure should be subject to continuous adaptations as conditions warrant.

Increasing Efficiency in Administration

Efficiency in administration essentially depends on the extent of observation of the basic principles of administration. Proper organisation of the administrative staff, recruitment of personnel of the required intellectual, moral and physical qualities and proper relations with public increase efficiency. In addition to these, if the following things are observed it increases the efficiency of the administration.

1) *Fixed Hours of Work*

This should be declared by the office and all should follow these timings. Irregularity and unpunctuality lead to laxity causing inconvenience to the public.

2) *Red Tapism*

It should be avoided. Too much rigidity in working or following the office routine leads to red tape. There should be provision for quick and important decision by setting aside the red tape.

3) *Delay*

Delay leads to corruption. Many times it occurs due to the

indecisiveness of the person handling the issue as he passes away time on some routine excuses. It should be avoided.

4) *Formalism*

It may not be insisted in all cases for increasing efficiency. It should be remembered that formal procedures of working are laid down for control and checking the work and not obstructing it.

5) *Obscurities*

Obscurities should be avoided in orders. Due to different interpretations it gives rise to disputes and confusion.

6) *Abuse of Power*

Abuse of power should be avoided. The human (peons, drivers, etc.) and non-human (office stationery, vehicles, etc.) resources of the office should be used for the purpose for which they are meant. It gives rise to anarchy in the administration.

Extension Organisation

Organisations are the assembling of two or more interacting human beings collectively seeking to attain some common goal. Organisations came into being when it became necessary to relate or coordinate the activities of the interacting human beings as they pursue a common goal.

The concept of organisation is further elaborated for organising resources. In addition to assembling human beings it also helps in organising resources. The assembling and arranging of the various resources available to the organisation is likely to result in the attainment of the stated objectives of the organisation. It also helps in clearly specifying the responsibilities, establishing the working relationships and developing policies to guide the use of such resources. Thus, organisation includes assembling of both human and non-human resources.

Normally the administration is run from the office of the organisation. Office is the seat at which the management of activities is initiated and centred. In the office there is generally a horizontal division of labour so that the head can see the business as a whole. He can also delegate the responsibility with matching authority to his subordinates. For the convenience of supervision and proper division of labour, the office is divided into different sections and sub-sections. The following is the suggested layout of the office.

1) *Registry and Recording Section*

This does the work of registering the particulars of receipts and despatch correspondence, filing and indexing.

2) *Subject Section*

Each subject or complaint within a subject are dealt with in these different sections.

3) *General Section*

This generalises or unifies the work of different sections and is directly under the head of the office.

4) *Finance and Account Section*

This looks after the financial aspect like budgeting, controlling expenditure and accounting of the funds received in the office.

5) *Establishment Section*

This looks after the management of the staff in terms of its recruitment, appointment, transfers, promotions and matters of discipline.

6) *Intelligence Section*

This deals with securing information and its interpretation. Reports, collection of data, research, statistics, etc., are some of the sources from which the information is collected.

The work of the office involves writing. This facilitates in keeping evidence, searching precedents and deliberations within outside the organisation. This is mostly done in the form of letters, notings, orders, rules and regulations. Common and relevant papers related to a particular issue are kept togcther in a file.

Technical Problems in the Building of an Organisation

A wide range of factors contribute to the unique form which

an organisational structure takes in a particular situation. The following six factors appear to be of special attention for building of an extension organisation.

1) *Increase in Size of Staff*

The organisation would expand and therefore there should be scope for its expansion. With the increase in staff, a higher degree of specialisation will occur. This calls for more coordination among organisational members. There will be greater need for delegating responsibility and authority for improving the skills in dealing with people and for giving constant attention to establishing and reestablishing the working relationships between and among the members. These and other factors substantially multiply the problems of organising human resources which daily confront administrators.

2) *Changes in Personnel*

Changes in the organisation often bring men with different philosophies of administration, different levels of knowledge and skill in administrative leadership, different concepts of the total range of objectives of the organisation and different perceptions of the resources needed to attain these objectives. The increased emphasis on specialisation among members has resulted in the chain reaction which must be taken into account while formulating an organisation. (a) Increasing desire by individual members to participate in organisational decisions and to engage in organisational problem-solving activity. (b) Increasing interest in being identified more closely with a sub-unit of the parent organisation such as the professional subject matter department, as well as being identified with the parent organisation. (c) Increasing interest in being closely associated with research. (d) Increasing degree of occupational mobility.

3) *Changes in Clientele*

Farm families are undergoing change and there has been an equally important development in terms of the type of assistance they need, particularly by commercial farmers who are producing the bulk of agricultural products. The level of formal education with whom we work is also increasing and it poses a challenge for the organisation to adjust with them.

4) *Changes in the Predominant Bases of Organisation*

There are three bases for organisation building. The first is functional in which the organisation arranges its staff according to the function to be assigned to them. In this an individual is administratively accountable to the functional superior. Secondly, the organisation building is on the basis of geographic area in which the assignment is according to specific geographic area. In this the individual is administratively accountable to the area incharge. Thirdly, on the basis of clientele in which the assignment is according to the specific part of the clientele, usually an occupational group (such as farm families) with administrative accountability to a clientele superior in the organisation.

5) *Changes in Objectives of the Organisation*

As the organisation grows it undergoes changes in terms of its objectives. The extension service in India started with the concept of the multipurpose worker (VLW) at the village level. It has undergone change and now there is thinking to appoint unipurpose workers at the lower level. The organisational structure will have to be modified as per the changes in the objectives of the organisation.

6) *Changes in Bases of Authority Available to Members of Organisation*

Authority is the process of influencing the behaviour of other people. Authority can be based on (a) law and administratively approved rules and regulations, (b) knowledge, often called the 'authority of know-how', (c) 'authority of position' —influence based on the use of power which elicits compliance and, (d) 'authority of the situation' which stems from the result of the group utilising the problem-solving process to make decisions. Historically it has been demonstrated that by pre-service and in-service training and by selective recruiting, members who choose to belong to an organisation can adapt themselves to any one of these forms of authority. While doing this, they develop intensive commitment to the organisation, which is most important for the good functioning of the organisation.

In addition to the other foregoing factors like the staffing training, morale, programme coordination, budgets and reports are important in building an organisation. Interagency relationships for obtaining technical information, staff-assistance and financial support are also becoming important concerns in the establishment of the organisation.

Salient Features of Extension Organization

The importance of separate extension organization is recognised in recent years. On the onehand such a organization has to maintain contacts with people and on the other hand it has to keep in touch with the subject matter specialists and other related input and service agencies. The extension job is educational in nature and hence democratic and persuasive approach is used in convincing the clientele.

The change agents working in the extension organization should know and understand the local situation. In other words the change agent has to be an area specialist i.e. he should know the environment in which new information or technology is required so that he can know the need of the new technology in a given situation. Most of these technology originates outside the extension organization and therefore, special linkages with the providers of information are required. This information need to be accurate and unbiased so as to establish the credibility of the organization. Extension needs a two-way flow of communication with both research personnel and its clientele. Extension work involves circular communication from the researcher through extension to the clientele with subsequent feedback to the researcher. As pointed out earlier the extension worker has to be in contact with the clientele, as the effectiveness of extension is directly related to number of contacts made by the extension worker with given individuals and the approach used by the extension worker. It is for this reason the extension worker need to have adequate and appropriate mobility in the area of his work. The extension organization cannot work in isolation and has to maintain contacts with entire agricultural and rural development sector. Rural and farm policies, farm prices, input availability and dependability all have critical bearing on an extension work. The extension organization need to have continuing interaction with external agencies, including sources of credit and inputs, as well as with marketing agencies and policy makers. These organizations need to be collaborated with the extension organization for effective extension work.

Functions of Extension Personal

There are several categories of staff created in the extension organization. This staff can be broadly classified into three categories namely, local or village extension workers (VEWS) who work directly with the clientele, Subject Matter Specialist (SMSs), who are responsible for training and providing technical expertise for VEWs, administrative and Supervisory staff, who are responsible for supervising VEWs and other staff as well as for carrying out the routine administrative functions.

The VEW is a last link between the extension organization and the farmers. He is expected to be a teacher, facilitator, organizer and leader at the village level. For performing these roles he should live and work in the geographic area where he is assigned. The VEW should not be assigned with regulatory functions. He should be assigned only educational and communication duties. Some of the functions, the local extension worker is expected to carryout include the following.

1) The VEW should develop a working relationship with all groups of farmers and other clientele in the community. He can accomplish this by paying regular visits to villages, farmers, demonstration sites and other places in his area. He should also cooperate with farmers, community leaders, dealers and other business people. He need to establish a liasion with people in general service area and other public agencies like, government, research agencies and educational institutions.

2) VEW should develop appropriate advisory mechanisms by establishing and participating in various committees. He should obtain local level input and feedback in programme development and implementation.

3) VEW should develop plans and prepare reports on extension activities carried out in the service area.

4) He should conduct educational activities such as demonstrations, meetings, surveys, field days, workshops and so forth for all the farmers. He should also help other agencies in

organizing exhibits, compaigns and other special projects.

5) Provide accurate and reliable information to all groups of farmers based on authoritative and unbiased source. He should assist as needed in preparing release for the press, radio and/ or television.

6) Cooperate fully with other staff members in the extension organization in planning, conducting and evaluating extension programmes.

Local extension workers are the area specialists and need the support of Subject Matter Specialists (SMSs). The SMSs are expected to provide a continuing flow of new technology and other research information to VEWs. In addition, there are other smaller groups of specialists such as communicators and trainers who provide essential support function.

In addition to the VEWs, and other support staff there is a need of the administrative and supervisory staff who are responsible for managing and organizing the programme by giving it leadership and direction. The administrative function includes planning, organizing, directing and controlling the activities of the organization. This has been elaborately dealt in the begining of this chapter.

Proper supervision of staff is a key element in developing effective extension work. In general supervision is important at each level but it is more important at the VEWs level. The Agricultural Extension Officers (AEOs) have this important responsibility. Individual guidance, encouragement and on the job councelling constitute important aspects of supervision.

Perception of Problems of Extension Organizations

Sigman and Swanson (1984) made a study of the problems perceived by Extension Directors in developing countries. The combined ranking of problems in order of importance of seriousness are presented here.

1) Mobility: Field level extension personnel lack adequate transportation to reach farmers efficiently.

2) Extension training: Extension personnel lack training in extension methods and communication skills.

3) Equipments: Extension personnel lack essential teaching and communication equipments.

4) Organizational tasks: Extension personnel are assigned with many other tasks besides extension work.

5) Technical training: Field-level extension personnel lack practical agricultural training about improved technology.

6) Teaching aids: Extension personnel lack essential teaching aids, bulletins, demonstration material and so forth.

7) Linkage: A continuing two-way flow of information between extension services and national agricultural research institutions is lacking.

8) Technological deficiencies: Appropriate technology is not available to extend to farmers.

In order to improve the working of extension organizations it is necessary to remove the above bottlenecks.

Extension Training

Extension personnel who enter the extension service should be prepared to perform basic extension tasks. The object of the trainings in extension is to help the personnel in understanding the philosophy and objectives of extension and technology to be transferred. The personnel who are on the job need to be trained in professional and technical competancies. The extension staff is trained by pre-service and inservice trainings for performing their jobs effectively.

Preservice Training

Preservice training is a programme of learning activities that prepares an individual for a career in extension, and usually leads to some type of diploma, certificate, degree or other qualification in one or more of the following—agriculture, fisheries, forestry, animal/veterinary science or home economics. In most of the countries the responsibility of implementing pre-service educational programme is with the State Agriculture Universities. The extension service should work closely with these institutions to influence pre-service training objectives and the approach pursued by these institutions.

Inservice Training

Inservice training is a planned programme of learning opportunities offered to staff members for purpose of improving the performance of individual in already assigned positions.

Induction/Orientation Training

Induction/Orientation training is offered at the time when new personnel are employed in the organization. The purpose of this training is to make new employers familiar with the practices and procedures of the organization. A good induction training will assist the new employers in developing a feeling that they are an important part of the organization, reduces the initial stress related to performance of the task, identify the resources available to support them in their role and strengthen their personnel commitment and dedication to the extension clientele through the extension organization., Normally this training is offered on the first day of employment.

The inservice trainings ensure that the field staff maintain their competancies throughout their careers. The major types of inservice trainings can be described as follows.

a) Trainings designed to correct deficiencies of new or promoted staff in their appropriate subject matter areas.

b) Bringing staff regularly up to date on new developments in their respective subject matter areas.

c) Training in the extension teaching methods that are necessary for success on the job.

Continuing education and career development is a life long process. In this process an individual alone or in a group consciously choose to engage in learning opportunities for the purpose of becoming more professional. Successful extension workers feel satisfied with the work they perform. They make efforts to design and develop plan for their own continuing education and professional development. This help in improving their professional competency and increasing the effectiveness and efficiency of the extension service. Some of the continuing education plans might include.

a) Academic course work beyond entry level degree programme.

b) Self-directed learning experiences with his or with others (study groups, quality circles etc.)

c) Professional association involvement.

All the above three categories support the individual and the organization.

CHAPTER 7

Rural Sociology and Community Organisation

Sociology is the scientific study of people in group relationships. Sociologists utilise scientific methods in their research studies to develop a body of accurate and reliable knowledge about human relationships. The contents or subject matter of sociology is not literary writing as is assumed by many people. It is a detailed and systematic study of society. There are animal societies also but sociology studies only human societies. Human beings have progressed to a large extent and therefore, sociology is used for the systematic study of the human beings in group relations. Secondly, sociology is concerned with people and without people or human beings, there cannot be any sociology. It cannot be in isolation as its main emphasis is on people. These people are not studied as individuals but rather in their relationship with other persons. They stay in groups and therefore the sociologists study people organised in families, friendship groups, temples, schools, industrial plants and in other organisations. In short, sociology studies the social behaviour of people, their different social groups, and the intra- and interrelationship of these social groups. Intrarelationship is the relationship of individuals within the group. Interrelationship is the relation of the groups among themselves.

Meaning

After knowing sociology, rural sociology should now be understood. Rural sociology is the systematic study of people living in rural areas and who are living by or are immediately dependent on agriculture. As stated earlier, sociology refers to man regardless of whether his residence is urban or rural. However, the majority of the people live in villages and rural areas and follow patterns of occupation and life somewhat different from those living in urban areas. The way of life they lead is influenced by their rural environment. Sociology is the scientific study of people in group relationships. In rural sociology the focus is on people living in rural areas.

Rural sociology is expected to develop greater understanding of the behaviour of rural people and rural society. In addition to providing scientific knowledge about rural society and laws governing its development, it should serve as a guide and suggest practical programmes of reform or construction of that society in the economic, social and cultural fields.

Scope

The scope of rural sociology is very wide as it studies the relationships and interactions in village society. However, rural sociology has to work at least in three areas. The first area of rural sociology is the accumulation of sociological knowledge and using it for solving the present problems of rural society. Secondly, rural sociology should direct its efforts in obtaining sociological knowledge by empirical research procedures. Thirdly, rural sociology has to channel its efforts by keeping faith in the methods used in this discipline in solving rural problems. It may work towards finding out new methods and procedures but there should be a belief in the minds of the rural sociologists that rural problems can be solved by these methods.

The studies in rural sociology include rural social psychology, rural social organisations and rural social values. All these aspects are of importance in developing programmes for improving rural life. Rural population is about two-thirds of the world population and lives mainly in developing countries. In India three-fourths of the population lives in villages and therefore, efforts are being made to improve the rural areas of the country. Most of the programmes like Five Year Plans, community development projects, integrated rural development programmes, etc., are launched by the government for bringing changes in rural areas.

Importance

After achieving independence the country had to face the task of tackling widely diverse problems of which acute food shortage was the main problem. The rapidly increasing population was to be fed by increasing food production which was among the lowest in the world. The main difficulty in this process was not the know-how of the new technology but the difficulty of communicating it to the farmers in an acceptable form. After communicating this scientific knowledge and skills, it was necessary to help the farmers in adopting it. Realising this difficulty, channels of communication were established by launching the National Extension Service in 1953. The change agents like village level workers were posted in villages for bringing about change in the village community. The efforts of the village level workers were coordinated at block and district levels. The change agents required sufficient technical knowledge and skill in the improved agricultural practices to be introduced among farmers. They also needed skill in communicating this knowledge of practices to the farmers.

Transfer or communication of innovations is the main job of these change agents. But for introducing improved farm practices, an effective strategy of approach based on a thorough knowledge and understanding of the farmer, his social and cultural environment within which he operates in his home, his village and the local region is necessary. Rural sociology provides such knowledge and makes possible the planning of a strategic approach for the desired changes. It allows constant analysis of the rural situation and within reasonable limits prediction of possible results.

From this point of view the main emphasis in the community development programmes is on changing human behaviour and working with rural people by using educational (democratic) methods. For doing this, as stated earlier, the change agent must have adequate knowledge and skill in methods of communication. In addition to this the change agent must know what is going on in the minds of rural people, thei relationships and interactions, their groups, their institutions, their organisations and the culture they share. All these factors influence the farmer's behaviour. The knowledge regarding these factors is provided by rural sociology. In the absence of this knowledge of rural society the change agent will not be able to plan a proper strategy of change. The change agent in the first instance has to understand the programmes and their objectives. Secondly, he must know the currents of thoughts in the minds of the people with whom he works. He needs to understand their motives, their reactions and their receptivity to new ideas. He should also understand why some people are more receptive than others, why some people take the initiative and lead and why others hesitate.

Thus an understanding of rural people and their life is essential for the change agent. Due to this he will be able to gain deep insight into the behaviour of rural people and the influence of their culture and society on them. He will also understand the human forces which can help and others that will put obstacles in his efforts. He will recognise the hidden resources of rural people and know which social and cultural obstacles to avoid rather than try to carry the programme across them. He will become aware of how much is known and how much is yet to be known about the behaviour of rural people.

Characteristics of Rural Society

Rural people are different from those living in urban areas. These differences are mainly due to the environment and its consequent impact on the personalities and the lives of the people. Here we are mainly interested in the characteristics of rural people. These characteristics are studied in relation to the urban people. Such rural-urban differences are discussed here.

1) *General Environment and Orientation to Nature*

The rural people are closely associated with nature as they live in that environment. They have to face the vagaries of nature like rains, heat, drought, etc. It has direct effect on their lives. Due to this they build up their beliefs and convictions about nature. These are different from that of the urban people.

2) *Occupation*

Most of the rural people depend on agriculture for their

livelihood. The non-agricultural jobs are few and are not of much economic importance. In urban areas most of the jobs are non-agricultural and more specialised. In a factory, the jobs of the foreman, manager and executive are different. A farmer on the other hand must be competent in a variety of skills—soil improvement, repairs to machine, skills in controlling pests and diseases, skills as animal husbandry—man and skills of agricultural economics as business manager as he handles the marketing, distribution, overall planning and operation of his farming enterprise. Farmers thus have to acquire a wide range of specialisation as compared to the urban workers.

3) *Size of Community*

The rural communities are smaller as compared to urban communities. The land to man ratio is higher in rural areas as most of the rural people depend on agriculture. The density of population per square mile is low as compared to urban areas.

4) *Homogeneity and Heterogeneity*

Homogeneity is the similarity of social and psychological characteristics in the population such as languages, beliefs, mores and patterns of behaviour. In this sense the rural population is more homogeneous. The urban population is more heterogeneous as it comprises persons from a wide variety of sub-cultures, interests, occupations and patterns of behaviour including language.

5) *Social Differentiation*

There are many urban services namely, educational, recreational, religious, business and residential. These are intentionally organised to serve specific purposes. These services have made the division of labour and differentiated the urban society as per the objective of the services. In contrast, rural society is more homogeneous in nature, relatively independent and with a low degree of social differentiation.

6) *Social Stratification*

Society is divided into high class and low class groups. The high class group is on the top of the ladder, the middle group is in the centre and the low class group is at the bottom. This gap between the high and low classes is more in urban areas as is evident from the wealthy and poor or palaces and slums. This range is not so wide in rural areas. Most of the rural society tends to belong to the middle class. The very rich and very poor move to the city. The rich move to the city as they desire to obtain more than what is provided by the rural areas. On the other hand, the poor move to urban areas in search of job opportunities, in order to supplement their income.

7) *Social Mobility*

It refers to the movement from one social group to another. It may be in the occupational mobility from one occupation to another, territorial mobility from rural to urban areas, from urban to rural areas or within the rural or urban areas. Social mobility is more from rural areas to urban areas. A series of both horizontal and vertical moves are seen in urban areas.

8) *Social Interaction*

The pattern and type of social interaction is different in urban and rural areas. The rural population is smaller and less dense than the urban population. The rural people have fewer personal contacts per individual. The contacts through various mass media like radio, television, magazines, posters, newspapers, etc., are lower in rural areas. The contacts in rural areas are more face to face, informal and personal. The urban contacts may be frequent but they tend to be more cursory, formal and impersonal.

9) *Social Control*

Informal social pressures act more as a means of social control in rural areas due to personal and informal contacts. Due to the small size and homogeneity of rural communities there is a more informal atmosphere in rural areas. In urban areas, control is more by formal, impersonal means of law-prescribed rules and regulations with penalties for violation.

10) *Leadership Pattern*

There is more fact-to-face contact in rural areas and hence the leadership is more on the basis of the personal traits of the leaders or their representatives. The leadership in urban areas is more impersonal.

11) *Social Solidarity*

There is more informal non-contractual personal relationships in rural areas. The cohesion and unity in rural areas is due to common traits, similarity of experience and common objectives which are shared by rural people. In urban areas unity and experience are based on differences and dissimilarities, division of labour, interdependence and socialisation. There is more impersonal, strictly formal and contractual kind of relationship.

This gap between the rural and urban differences is being narrowed due to the communication of new ideas and the extension of service facilities to rural areas. A complete closure of this gap will not be possible in the near future. However, questions are being raised regarding the desirability of urbanising the rural area. Instead of this the recent approach is on modernising the rural area, in which effort is made to utilise the rural environment to benefit the rural people without altering the rural scene to a great extent. Effort is being made to strike an ecological balance in rural areas.

Rural Social Groups

A man is born in a social group. He grows and relates himself to groups by interacting with them in various ways. He first comes in contact with his mother, and the family members. As he grows he goes out and plays with the neighbouring children. Then he goes to the school and participates in that group as a member of the school class. His group contacts are widened as he develops and assumes various roles as a member of society. These groups influence his attitudes, thinking and behaviour throughout his life. They deeply influence the development of his personality and play a vital role in his socialisation.

A social group is a unit of two or more persons in reciprocal interaction or communication with each other.

At least two persons should come together to form a group who are capable of exchanging their thoughts. However a mere coming together of people does not form a group. There should be communication and interaction among them. Communication means sharing of common experiences and interaction by means of exchanging meaningful gestures (words, smiles, signs, frowns or yawns) among each other. Two persons sitting physically close to one another may not form a group when they do not interact. On the other hand two persons talking on telephone form a group as they interact with each other. The communication and interaction should not be one way but it should be from both the persons. This is called reciprocal or two-way communication and interaction. The communication need not be 'face to face' but may be through telephone, letter, radio or other suitable communication media.

The group lives together as long as there is reciprocal psychological interaction. Groups cease to be groups when active relation between the minds of the two or more involved ceases. The family functions as a group till its members are in reciprocal interaction for a period of time. The family is separated when this interaction ceases. Common interests shared values and norms is the essential part of the social group. This may not be true for all the groups. Members with divergent views may come together for some time and interact for agreement or disagreement. They may not share a common purpose and yet may engage in strenuous reciprocal interaction on a psychological plane.

Social groups are classified from different angles. No single classification is applicable to all social groups. Major social groups as classified by eminent sociologists are presented in the following paragraphs.

Primary and Secondary Groups

The persons in the primary group have face-to-face relationships, such as a family and a play group. A secondary group is one where the relationships are indirect. The members of a secondary group have little personal affection and their relationships are governed by the fulfilment of some objective. The specific characteristics of primary and secondary groups are compared here.

Primary group	Secondary group
1. Small in size, mostly less than 20 to 30 persons are members.	1. Large in size.
2. Personal and intimate relationship among the members.	2. Indirect relationships with little personal affection.
3. Face to face contact.	3. Contact through mostly other communication media.
4. Mostly permanent membership	4. Temporary membership.
5. Relations among members are mostly informal.	5. The relations are mostly formal.

In urban societies secondary relationships are more as compared to the rural society. Primary groups like friends and relatives, directly influence the behaviour of the individual. The impersonal nature of relationship in the secondary group like producer and salesman or workers in big organisations makes for the absence the bondage which the primary relations have.

Formal and Informal Groups

This is a classification of groups according to the mode of organisation and functioning of the group. As the name indicates the formal groups have procedures of functioning. These groups have (1) a name or title, (2) selected and titled officers, (3) a written purpose, and (4) a regular, common, meeting time and place. Informal groups like friends, group of a neighbourhood do not have any such characteristics. There is no organisation or rules. The members have maximum freedom to think and act. The formal groups such as village councils, farmer's societies and school committees have definite rules of operation. This discipline of action gives stability to these groups, whereas the informal groups can break at any time.

Reference Groups

Every person in society has his reference group. It is a group of persons whom an individual consults before taking an important decision. A reference group, therefore, may contain members from the primary group, informal group or formal group. In complex societies a person can be a member of different reference groups. But in communities like a village a person has a specific reference group. The decisions taken in consultation with a reference group naturally influence the behaviour of the member. Sometimes a person may not be a so-called member of any reference group but he may consult a group of experienced and respected persons in society and take decisions according to their advice.

Cultural Interest Group

These groups are created for the development of special interests. They are formed on account of factors such as economic interest, technical interest, religious interest, intellectual interest, aesthetic interest, political, educational or recreational interest.

Temporary and Permanent Groups

The groups assembled for a short period are called temporary groups. The examples of such a group are crowd, mob, herd, etc.

The groups living in a geographical area for a longer period are called permanent groups. The examples are community, state, region, tribe, etc.

Informal Rural Institutions

A group of persons organising themselves for the purpose of fulfilling certain interests is known as an association. It is obvious that there can be many associations functioning in a community. Associations are organised for particular purposes. For instance, farmer's associations may be for the purpose of the sale of goods, a club for recreation or bhajan mandal for the purpose of worship. The associations are the means or agencies through which their members fulfil their common needs. Associations are organised and have office bearers to control the functioning of the associations.

Associations which have set procedures and rules of functioning are called institutions. A college is an association of students and lecturers but the educational system is an institution. A housing society is an association of persons interested in building houses of their own but it's functioning on a cooperative basis is an institution. Thus if we are considering something as an organised group it is an association but when it has certain fixed forms or procedures, it is an institution. Association denotes membership while institution denotes a mode or means of service. In the long run associations take the form of institutions. The community sets up certain institutions such as the celebration of festivals, mode of expressing joy and sorrow on specific occasions, mode of recreation, etc.

In short, an institution can be defined as an organised system of social relations which embodies certain common values and procedures and meets certain basic needs of society.

There are three major rural institutions namely family, class and caste.

Family

The family is the primary institution of society. It is the most multifunctional of all institutions. It is a system of organised relationships involving workable and dependable ways of meeting basic social needs. More specifically the family commonly fulfils the following functions in society:

1) Sex regulation.

2) Reproduction and perpetuation of the family and human race.

3) Socialisation.

4) Provision of economic maintenance and livelihood in many cultures.

5) Provision of love, affection and security to the individual.

6) Provision of class status to the individual, of the family into which he has been born.

There are secondary institutions in the family namely engagement, marriage, courtship and relationships with the family into which marriage has taken place.

The specific ways in which these functions are carried out are defined by the culture of the society concerned. There are mainly two types of families namely the conjugal (nuclear) family consisting of husband, wife and children and the consanguine (joint) family founded on blood relations of a large number of people and consisting of a large group of blood relatives with a fringe of spouses. Secondly, the number of persons united in the marriage may vary according to the system prevalent in the culture, namely monogamous (one man to one wife), polyandrous (one woman to more than one man), or polygamous (one man to more than one woman). The family may be matrilocal (matri=mother, and local=place) in which the couple move in with the bride's parents after the wedding ceremony. The family can be patrilocal (patri=father and local= place) in which the newly weds reside with the groom's parents. The family can also be neolocal when the newly wed couple set up a separate residence and live with neither the wife's nor the husband's parents.

The family in India and in other parts of the world is in process of change, and many functions of the family have been transferred to other institutions in society. The family has tremendous influence on the individual, his behaviour and his actions. It moulds him from childhood and has a significant influence on the development of his personality.

Class

The term social class may not be new to most of the students. The terms richer class, middle class and poor class are often used, rather closely for the sake of understanding. The significance of the term varies from a statistical or social category like old and young, men and women to one of the strongly social-conscious groups like caste.

Social classes are defined as abstract categories of persons arranged in levels according to the social status they possess. There are no firm lines separating one category from the other. Classes are loosely organised groupings, whose members behave towards each other as social equals.

There is a marked distinction between class and group. Many a times while referring to age classes it is wrongly spoken as age group. In fact it is not a group but a statistical category. It sometimes assumes a class significance. This distinction will become more clear from the types of social classes described later. The classes may be based on power, prestige, wealth or a combination of these and other factors.

1) Defined classes are culturally defined groups recognised as such by society, e.g., tribal and nontribal classes.

2) Cultural classes are further social strata that have developed subcultural patterns of behaviour. The patterns are distinguished from each other, e.g., Mohammedan and Hindu cultural classes.

3) Economic classes are groups engaged in different economic activities or standing in different relationships to the means of production in a society, e.g., business, service, farmer and other classes.

4) Political classes are groups formed on the basis of political power, eg., Congress (I), Janata, Bharatiya Janata Party, etc.

5) Self-identified classes are conceived in terms of the identification of their members, e.g., Rotary Club, Lions Club, etc.

6) Participation classes are described in terms of the identification of social ties between the members. These social ties are sociable contacts, marriages and similar relationships in which the class as a whole participates ,e.g., village people participating in a religious function.

Caste

Caste is a social category whose members are assigned a permanent status within a given social hierarchy and whose contacts are restricted accordingly. It is the most rigid and clearly graded type of social stratification and has been often referred to as the extreme form of a closed class system: An individual is born into the caste of his parent and can rise no further. With few exceptions he cannot fall to a lower caste, but if he does violate taboos and other mores of his caste he may be ostracised and expelled from his caste group. Personal qualities or ability have no part whatever in determining the caste of an individual, with lineage being the only criterion. The following are the characteristics of a rigid caste system.

1) Membership in the caste is hereditary and unchangeable for life.

2) Marriages must be made within the caste line.

3) Contact with other castes or sub-castes in all aspects of life is strictly regulated and limited by the mores.

4) There is a caste name and often a traditional caste occupation. Each caste has its particular customs, and control over the individual is exercised by his caste.

5) The hierarchy of castes is well understood and strictly enforced according to its local variations.

The Hindu caste system had originally a four-fold division of society into (i) Brahmans (priests), (ii) Kshatriyas (rulers, nobles and soldiers), (iii) Vaishyas (commoners), and (iv) Sudras (servile classes). These castes were further subdivided into many subcastes.

Formal Rural Institutions

It is said that the dream of democracy will be brought into reality by three basic institutions in every village, namely, the panchayat, the cooperative society and the school. There has to be an organic link between each of these institutions. Each of them would be performing its activities within its own spheres and by taking interest in the affairs of the other. Each institution has therefore, to see how it can help the other two institutions in bringing about an integrated approach to solving local problems.

Village School

There is a natural bondage between the school and the community. It is in the home that the child is first introduced to the social life and till his fifth year the home functions exclusively as the child's school. Here the unconscious process of education is closely associated with the gradual growth of the child. In ancient India the boy used to be sent to the gurukula or ashram where he used to live with his guru and get in tune with the ashram life. All the activities in the ashram including the sishya's services for the guru were directed towards one goal and that was the education of the disciple.

This gurukula or ashram besides being the centre of education was also a centre of spiritual training for the pupils. Under the Buddhist system of education the ashrams became the centre of learning. These centres of learning were satisfying the requirements of the community. The education was not purely intellectual but it took note of the requirements of the community. The education imparted to Kshatriyas and Vaishyas included the study of Vedas and other technical skills required in the community. The Vaishya was acquainted with the manner of sowing the seeds and of the good and bad qualities of fields. He has to know all measures and weights, and was able to judge the excellence and defects of commodities, the knowledge of different countries, the probable profit and loss on merchandise and the means of properly rearing cattle.

During the Muslim rule in India the system of education underwent a lot of changes. Mosques were established all over the country and it was the centre of literary activity. In many cases the maulvi of the mosque was the teacher.

During the British rule many changes were introduced into the educational system. Up to this time the school teacher was a dynamic figure in the villages. School was the integral part of the community. The student was in intimate touch not only with students but also with the village community, as a whole. But with the establishment of the foreign rule and the consequent administrative set-up, the school lost its intimacy with the villagers. With the introduction of the foreign language, education became further removed from the needs of the community.

It was Gandhiji who first gave serious thought to this decline of the role of the school teacher in the village community. He enunciated a new programme called basic education to rectify the defects in the educational system. The forces realised by Gandhiji through basic education were strengthened by another movement, the community development programme. Basic education prepared the child to become a full man, the creation of which is the goal of community development. In this context, the school has to assume a major responsibility in the development of the community. The role formerly played by the school and the school teacher in the village community has now to be restored.

In order to revitalise the school as a community centre, the school may undertake the following activities:

a) Cultural and community activities
b) Physical education activities and sports activities
c) Organising youth welfare activities
d) Literacy activities

e) Scouting, sevadal and other social welfare movements
f) Conduct of exhibitions and campaigns
g) Organising school cooperatives
h) Organising museums and development of aesthetic sense
i) Organising tours and excursions.

In addition to these the following activities would bring a closer relationship between the school and the village community:

a) Parent teacher's association
b) The school betterment committee
c) Observance of mother's day (for mothers of school children)
d) Celebration of birthdays
e) Celebration of birthdays of eminent personalities.

The local panchayat and youth club can assist the school in certain activities such as fencing the school gardens, supplying saplings for schools, sinking and cleaning of wells within the premises of the schools, maintenance of school gardens especially during vacations, while the teacher associated with the activities organised by the village community and who undertakes the responsibility of organising certain functions at the school, must see that such activities do not hamper the regular curriculum of the school.

The school teachers have to organise the school community in such a way that it will be a model of the future village community. The school may render all possible help to the voluntary organisations like youth mandal, mahila mandal, bhajan mandal, etc., when they undertake any programme which is useful for the village community. The school teacher must try to promote the growth of these voluntary organisations in the village.

In short, the teacher should act as a friend, philosopher and guide to the villagers in all extension programmes. He has to play a prominent part by cooperating with the field extension workers.

Grampanchayat

It was considered that India's independence must begin at the base. Every village should be republic or a grampanchayat having full powers. By utilising these powers the grampanchayats will be able to give better service to the villagers. The panchayats were in existence as early as the Vedic age. The word gramini is referred to it in the Vedas. It means the leader of the village. There is a reference to Janpadas in Valmiki's Ramayana which were a kind of federation of village republics. In the Mahabharat and Manusmriti, there is a mention of gramsanghs. Panchayat rule was in existence even during the times of Mauryas. These gramsabhas continued to flourish till the British appeared on the Indian scene. Even though empires rose and fell, the panchayats survived. They retained their autonomous character and continued to function in spite of political changes, thereby helping to preserve democratic traditions in the social, cultural and economic life of the people. With the coming of the British, the process of commercialisation of agriculture for exports started. There was also linking up of the upper part of the caste structure in the village to a caste economy. This has disrupted the community life of the village. In consequence the villages lost their self-sufficient character.

Efforts to revive these panchayats were made in 1935 by introducing a comprehensive Village Panchayat Act in several states, in India. The panchayats gained more prominence, after independence but the real credit for the revitalisation of the panchayats goes to the committee on planned projects known as the Balwantrai Mehta Committee (1957). The committee recommended a three tier system of administration for the district, in which the panchayats occupied the bottom place.

There is historical evidence to show that in ancient India the panchayats enjoyed large powers. For instance, they made arrangements for the defence of the community, settled disputes in the villages and organised works of public utility and recreation. They collected taxes on behalf of the central government and levied their own. They even acted as trustees and bankers and raised public loans to mitigate the hardships of famines. The panchayats also ran schools and poor houses, and raised funds for them, in addition to supervising the religious activities of the temples. They had adequate public funds at their disposal for the discharge of these functions. The functions visualised for the panchayats in the Panchayat Acts cover administrative, municipal and socio-economic activities at the village level. Generally separate panchayats have been entrusted with judicial functions.

The Village Panchayat Act 1958 can broadly be distinguished under three categories, namely, (i) the Act which largely confers municipal functions and in some states limited judicial powers; (ii) the Act which includes economic and development functions as optional, and (iii) the Act which gives equal priority to economic and developmental functions.

The panchayat can thus undertake a wide range of activities. These include public health and sanitation, water supply, street lighting, maternity and child welfare, the registration of births and deaths, fire service and watch and ward in the villages. The provision of education and recreation and the construction and maintenance of village roads, tanks, wells, bunds, etc., also come within the purview of the panchayats, as also relief to the poor, the destitutes and the victims of floods and famines and the removal of untouchability. They can also attend to the development of agriculture, the improvement of livestocks, the promotion of cottage and rural industries and the setting up of rural cooperatives.

An important function of the panchayats concerns the administration of justice. They have been empowered to try civil suits involving small amounts, as well as minor criminal cases, such as those relating to theft, simple hurt, cattle treas-pass, public gambling, etc.

To enable the panchayat to play its role as the basic organisation for planning development, welfare, land reform and land management at the village level, the Planning Commission recommended that the existing legislation should be amended, where necessary, with a view to vesting the panchayats with the following new functions, namely, (i) to draw up production for the execution of the programmes, (ii) to frame budgets for the execution of the programmes, (iii) to act as the channel through which government assistance should increasingly reach the villages, (iv) to bring waste land under cultivation, (v) to arrange for the cultivation of fallow land, (vi) to organise voluntary labour for community schemes, (vii) to arrange for the cooperative management of land and other resources, and

(viii) to implement measures for land reform.

In addition to this, more emphasis is given to the role of grampanchayat in accelerating the rate of agricultural development. It is considered that agricultural development is the basis for other development in the village. In the modern age, agricultural development cannot be brought about by farmers acting alone. In order to increase agricultural productivity, the farmer now depends less and less on the natural resources of the farm and more and more on resources from outside. Agriculture cannot develop beyond the subsistence stage without appropriate developments in other parts of the community within which it is carried on. This role can be appropriately played by the grampanchayats.

Definite facilities and services must be available in the local community—the grampanchayat—if agriculture is to develop. Each of these is essential, without any one of them there can be little or no agricultural development.

The five essentials which must be available within the grampanchayat are:

1) Irrigation—the amounts of water and water control must be adequate for the types of crops grown.

2) Fertilisers, seeds, farm implements, supplies.

3) Open markets capable of absorbing the farmer's production at a profit to the farmer.

4) Adequate feeder roads connecting towns.

5) Efficient farming practices.

With the essentials assured, agriculture can progress. But progress will be accelerated if other organised activities are also available within the grampanchayat. These activities include, education for development, production credit, group action by farmers, basic improvements in farm land plus bringing new land into cultivation, and local plans for agro-industrial development.

Since the accelerators are useless if even one of the essentials is missing, it does not pay to devote scarce manpower and financial resources in a given area to any programme to accelerate agricultural development until the essentials are provided.

But where the essentials are available, the following programmes can be initiated and coordinated within the grampanchayat in order to achieve agricultural development.

1) Local tests to determine the yields and profitability of suggested new farm practices.

2) Demonstrations of new practices on the fields of selected farmers.

3) Farm tours so that more farmers can get acquainted with new practices.

4) Extension teaching to help farmers to carry out new practices successfully.

5) Credit programmes of finance supplies needed in modern farming.

6) Farmers' associations or other means of group action.

The task of grampanchayat planning for agricultural development is to make sure that the essentials are available within the grampanchayat and to coordinate the programmes for accelerating agricultural development.

Service Cooperatives

Cooperation started with human life itself. When human beings began to associate with each other cooperation came into existence. The principle of cooperation was realised since Vedic days in India. 'Let us help each other and take up the right path in life' was the preaching of the great saint Ramdas. He advised the people to do good things with each other's help.

Every individual tries to seek happiness and one of the ways of achieving happiness is with the help of money. So people started coming together to achieve economic gains. This gave a new direction to cooperation. Cooperation has become one aspect of the vast movement which promotes voluntary associations of individuals having common needs and who combine towards the achievements of common economic ends.

The principle of cooperation was brought into practice through cooperative societies. The cooperative society is an association of an unlimited number of persons formed on the basis of equality for the promotion of member's interests and managed by the members themselves. The major development in the cooperative field since independence was on the basis of the Rural Credit Survey Committee report by the Reserve Bank of India (1954). The committee recommended an integrated scheme of rural credit involving three fundamental principles, namely, (1) state participation at different levels, (2) coordination of credit with other economic activities, and (3) administration through trained and efficient personnel. The committee expressed its view that at the village level Primary Credit Society is the only suitable organisation. But for carrying out its functions effectively and for fulfilling its aims it should be reorganised into a bigger unit covering a group of villages and employing a full-time qualified secretary. The committee also recommended open membership for all persons living in the villages.

The National Development Council in 1959 recommended radical reforms in the pattern of organisation of cooperative societies at the village level. It recommended that the organisation of cooperative societies should be on the basis of the village community and it should stress on increasing agricultural production. As per the recommendations of this committee the policy of organising large-sized societies like service cooperatives was introduced.

The service cooperatives are expected to cater to the needs of the farmers. The farmers require a large number of services other than credit, such as supply of seeds, fertilisers and insecticides for increasing agricultural production. The service cooperatives were to serve as a store, a bank, a distribution agent, a supply and marketing unit for the members. In other words these societies are expected to act as 'production promoting units' for its members.

For the development of the village community the service cooperatives should be treated as an organisation of the villagers for mutual help and cooperation to meet their common economic requirements and to increase agricultural production. Thus service cooperatives are expected to perform the following functions for the economic development of the village.

1) Advancing loans for the purchase of farm requirements and other industrial and agricultural purposes.

2) Arranging the supply of farm requirements such as improved seeds, fertilisers, insecticides, implements, etc.

3) Providing storage and marketing for the agricultural produce of members.

4) Maintenance and supply of agricultural machinery like plant protection equipment, threshers, cane crushers, etc. to members on hire.

5) Supplying essential commodities like sugar, kerosene oil etc., to members.

6) Providing technical guidance to the members in matters of agriculture for increasing agricultural production.

7) Mobilising the savings of the people to meet the above-mentioned requirements.

Thus the cooperatives are considered as a pivot of village economy and without cooperatives a village cannot progress economically. The management of the cooperative societies should set an example to the rest of the community by efficient organisation and selfless service for the common people.

There are certain voluntary organisations in addition to the aforementioned which can play a vital role in the development of the village. Two of them, namely, mahila mandals and youth clubs are described here.

Mahila Mandals

Agriculture is a family enterprise. All members of the family, men, women and children are therefore involved in the process of increased production. The woman, in addition to her traditional responsibilities for the care of the family, also performs certain agricultural tasks, which are exclusively women's work. The care of buffalo, sheep, poultry and pigeons is entirely the responsibility of the housewife in many rural areas. The income she earns from the sale of butter, milk, eggs and other products helps to determine the food and the household items the family can afford. Efforts to raise the standard of village life or to increase the amount of animal protein available to the total population must teach the village women better agricultural and marketing practices.

In addition to these the rural women need to be helped in spending the additional income in the interest of better health and a higher living standard. Such type of education should include better use of local foods, their preservation, storage and preparation, home improvements with special emphasis on sanitation, safety and comfort, childcare and simple home crafts. The education will also help in correcting inadequate and improper feeding, contamination of food and water, and improper care of sick persons.

This education to the rural women should be given through

mahila mandals. The mahila mandals are independent voluntary organisations of local women. The purpose of the mandals is to educate the rural women in the activities stated earlier.

Youth Clubs

The rural development programmes would be effective when it has sound, competent and enlightened leadership. There is obvious need for training local leaders and preparing them to take their place in the development programmes. Youth work can solve this problem to some extent. The training of young people in club work will prepare them for future responsibilities. These trained young farmers will grow up as scientific farmers, with responsibilities of helping their brethren to change their attitudes and to take up new practices in farming and living. Thus efforts should be made towards the development of young farmers by organising and encouraging the formation of young farmers' clubs (youth clubs). The organisation of these clubs and other activities among the village youth would act as a process for the training of future village leaders.

Village Leaders

The objective of the rural development programme is to devolop peoples' participation. Therefore, it is essential to encourage and train village leaders who will develop effective working relationships with the rural people. The well-recognised method of working with the rural people is through these leaders. The leaders may be good or bad, progressive or constructive but they guide village thinking and lead them to action. The formal and informal village groups function through these recognised leaders. There are limitations in working alone by the extension worker. If he relies on individual contacts then he cannot greatly multiply his efforts. If he works through village leaders then the ideas spread quickly among the group and village.

Identification of Leaders

The existing popularly elected leaders like sarpanchas or panchayat members and office bearers of cooperative societies should be recognised and used in extension work wherever possible. The extension workers should also seek to discover and develop new leaders. The new situation will produce new leaders. The best way to find out the potential new leaders is by asking a number of villagers. A problem may be posed to the villagers. Then they may be asked the names of the persons who would be effective in solving that problem by organising them and by carrying out the necessary steps in solving that problem. If it is an important job the villagers will concentrate on naming one or two people.

It is said that there are one-tenths leaders and nine-tenths followers. So there will be no dearth of natural leaders. If the villagers gain experience in self-help development new leaders will emerge out of new situations.

Leadership Phenomena

After developing the leaders it is necessary to plan the ways to use them for development. It is especially important to be watching for young leaders, helping them into the leadership responsibility as they develop. Working through village institutions like panchayats, cooperatives, etc., will provide growth opportunities for village leaders. The village leaders will appreciate and work more if they are recognised by the village and extension workers. For giving recognition they should be kept in the fore-front when there are visits by the officials or other outside visitors. If the village leader is recognised then he will exert with renewed effort. This good functioning of the natural leaders will accelerate the rate of rural development.

Development of Leaders

For effective functioning of the leaders it will be necessary to train them after their identification. One of the ways to do this is by involving them in situations where they will have learning experiences. In the village meetings or at other such congregations the leaders may be encouraged to tell what the village has done and how it has been accomplished.

Tours for the village leaders may be planned within the panchayat samiti as well as to outside places where they can observe the rural development work in action. Training camps can be organised for the village leaders, block leaders and extension workers from time to time. There should be ample opportunity for these leaders to exchange their experiences and learn from each other, and from the block technical staff the progress achieved and problems encountered in improving all phases of village life. Where one village may have failed another may have succeeded. This exchange of ideas will help in analysing what various villagers have done, how they have approached their problems and with what degree of success. By going through these experiences the development of the leaders will take place.

Rural Community Organisation

Community organisation is a process by which a community identifies its needs, orders these needs, develops the confidence and will to work at them, finds resources to deal with them, and in doing so, extends and develops cooperative and collaborative attitudes and practices in the community.

In this definition, community organisation is considered as a process involving the total community in identifying and solving problems. Community means the people living in a specific geographic area (e.g. village, city or panchayat samiti). It includes groups of people, sharing common interests or functions, (e.g., welfare or education).

The process of identifying its needs or objectives is locating the problems of the community and focussing them. It helps in clarifying and defining the problems so that goals for community achievement can be set. The community orders or ranks these needs by certain criteria. It is almost impossible to deal with all the problems of society and hence it is necessary to deal with them one by one. This can be done by arranging them in order of priority. After identifying and focussing the problems the next step is to develop confidence and the will to work towards the needs among the community. Many times the community identifies the problems but the members of the community feel incompetent to deal with the objectives and feel that the objectives are beyond their reach. In these cases the change agents need to provide stimulation, encouragement and support to the community in developing their conviction that something can be done to solve their problems.

Finding the resources, internal or external to deal with these problems involves the discovery of tools, instruments, persons, techniques and material. In certain cases it is necessary to take outside help to solve the problems of the community. The community should be able to utilise fully its own resources, and at the same time recognise the points at which outside help or action can be obtained.

While taking action in solving the problems of the community, emphasis needs to be given to cooperative and collaborative attitudes and practices. It means that the process of community organisation should develop the will to understand, accept and work with one another. This, will reduce the conflicts and difficulties as the members will solve them by coming together.

In short, the objective of the community organisation is to develop the community in terms of its capacity to function as a unit in respect to its needs, problems and common objectives. This process of community organisation has two aspects, namely, planning and community integration. Planning involves the stages in identification of the problem to action in respect to it. Community integration is increasing the cooperative and collaborative attitudes and practices in the community. It is also known as community morale.

Principles of Community Organisation

The main emphasis in community organisation is in involving people in formulating and solving their problems. The principles given here are the elaboration of this view. It is believed that, if the organisations develop in a community, it will also develop the community.

1) *Start from the Felt Needs of Community*

The process of community organisation should start from the felt needs of the community. The community must feel unhappy (discontent) with the existing situation and should feel that it should be changed. It is just like the proverb 'necessity is the mother of inventions'. This situation is similar to one prevalent in psychiatry where pain is considered as a prerequisite to change.

2) *Discontent Needs to be Focussed*

The discontent among the community alone will not lead to the organisation of the community. This discontent needs to be focussed on something specific. It needs to be channelised into organisation, planning and action in respect to the specific problems.

3) *Discontent Must be Understood by the Community*

The discontent should not be limited to a smaller group in the community. The feeling of discontent must be recognised and understood by the major parts of the community. If the discontent is limited to a very small group then it will be a minority movement in which the whole community will not be interested.

4) *Community Leaders Should be Involved*

It is considered necessary to involve the people of the community in the process of community organisation. This is possible when the leaders (formal and informal) of the community are identified, accepted and involved in the organisation. These leaders represent major subgroups in the community and when they are involved in the organisation their followers feel that they are being represented through their leaders.

5) *Clarify Organisational Goals and Working Procedures*

The organisation will not continue effectively unless it has goals and methods of procedure which are acceptable to a majority of the community. The community has diversified groups with their interests, attitudes and behaviour patterns. These diversified groups will stay together if they find some common goals and methods to achieve these goals in the organisation. It is therefore, imperative to evolve certain common purposes for the existence of the group.

6) *Develop Sense of Belonging among Members*

The members of the organisation should feel a sense of belonging. For this purpose the programmes of the organisation should include some activities with emotional content. The organisation develops strength and cohesion through friendship, mutual support, difficult tasks, gay times, hardship, conflict and celebrations. The organisation arranges situations in which the community is brought together. This is mostly done on celebration and festive occasions. These activities provide rich emotional experiences and act as a binding mortar of the common sentiments in the community.

7) *Use Latent Goodwill of Members*

In every community there are good people who are interested in working for the welfare of the community. It should not be always considered that all the people are apathetic and indifferent towards the community welfare. This latent goodwill should be utilised by the organisation for the development of the community.

8) *Develop Proper Communication Channels*

In the modern world communication has gained a lot of importance. Communication is not only transmitting and receiving messages from sender to receiver but developing areas of common understanding and shared values among the members of the community. Faulty communication leads to misunderstanding. The organisation must develop active and effective lines of communication both within the organisation and between the organisations and the community. The organisation should develop an atmosphere in which the participants should feel free to express themselves.

9) *Seek Support of Different Groups*

There will be a number of organisations in the community. These different units will make the community a strong cohesive group. Community life cannot be separated from the life of these different parts. The change agent should seek to support and strengthen the groups which he tries to bring together in cooperative work

10) *Have Permanence with Flexibility in Decision-making*

The organisation should be flexible without losing its permanent regular decision-making routines. This is not to suggest that the established procedures of work should be often violated. It suggests that depending on the nature of problem at hand certain changes may be made for the smooth and quick working of the organisation. The organisation should not be a victim of red-tape.

11) *Adjust Pace of Work with Community*

The capacities of the communities differ in terms of their adjustment with the changing environment. It is, therefore, necessary to adjust the pace of life which exists in a particular community to keep up the tempo of the community programme. Secondly, the organisation should develop a pace of work by taking into account its resources.

12) *Develop Effective Leadership*

In the process of community organisation there is an involvement of the people through their leaders. The organisation should seek to develop effective leadership in the community. These leaders will contribute to the development of morale in the organisation and the community.

13) *Develop Collaborative and Cooperative Attitudes*

The process of community organisation is expected to develop a collaborative and cooperative attitude among the community. While doing this the organisation can become a symbol of loyalty and community cooperation. This will develop strength, stability and prestige in the community. One can have an idea of the community from the organisations and the way the organisations function. The organisations must have strength both in terms of its involvement of accepted group leaders and in terms of its ability to handle difficult community problems.

Methods of Community Organisation

There are three methods of community organisation. These methods are based on certain objectives which the community intends to fulfil.

1) *Specific Content Method*

In this method an individual, an agency, or an organisation becomes concerned about some needed reform in the community and launches a programme to secure this reform. Here the efforts are directed at the single goal of securing the reform or objective which the original individual, agency or organisation had in mind. The success of this method tends to be measured in terms of the degree to which the reform, goal or objective is achieved, e.g. the construction of a school building.

2) *General Content Method*

In this method the objectives of a group, association or council (such as panchayat samiti) is the coordination and orderly development of service in a particular area of interest. In this method the effort is made to coordinate the existing services, to extend the present services, and to initiate new services to meet the welfare needs of the community. The objective is not a single reform but a more general objective of effective planning and operation of a special group of services in the community. Mostly, the representatives of the different organisations are brought together in the process of decision-making. This involvement of the power figure in the planning process helps in coordinating the activities.

3) *Process Method*

In this method the emphasis is not on the content but on the initiation and nourishment of a process in which all the people of a community are involved, through their representatives, identifying and taking action in respect to their own problems. The idea is to develop a cooperative and collaborative attitude among various groups in the community. The aim of this method is to develop the capacity of the community in dealing with problems which arise in their community. The stress in this method is on involvement of the major subgroups of the community through their leaders in identifying their problems and utilising their energies in solving them. This method is slow but its effects are long-lasting as the community learns to solve its problems by utilising its own resources.

ENVIRONMENT

Environment is anything surrounding an object. Human beings are surrounded by many conditions which affect human life. It is essential to study the conditions which govern the life in a given situation before undertaking the programme of improvement. The conditions in which the life survives is studied under environment.

The environment can be broadly classified into four types. The natural environment, artificial environment, social environment and psycho-social environment. The details of each type of environment is described here.

1) Natural Environment: It is composed of those external objects or phenomena, which are beyond human capacity to control. There are two major divisions of these objects, i.e. physical and biological.

a) Physical Environment: The physical environment includes the natural objects such as soil, mountains and lakes; some resources like mineral mines, oil wells and physical agencies like sunshine, winds and moving water. The physical environment sets the condition in which man has to live. It depends upon the human society to prosper by utilising the physical resources of nature.

Utilisation of upper layer of earth crust (soil) is an example of how the human beings have adopted to nature's resources. Human beings have developed a system of cultivation of plants on the soil according to its capacity to provide nourishment to the crop plants. The variation in the soil fertility has resulted in economic disparities among the cultivators and regions.

The pressure of increasing human population is mounting high on the existing natural resources, like land available for cultivation, oil wells and coal mines. In the later half of the 20th century, farming has undergone tremendous changes with the introduction of hybrid varieties, chemical fertilizers and insecticides. The climate includes temperature rain fall and wind. Climate creates conditions which are beyond human control. Variations in temperature from chilling cold to boiling hot, some times pose a threat to human existence. The houses are built according to region's climatic conditions, so as to provide comfortable living conditions. The seasonal variations in temperature and rainfall have great impact on human living.

Monsoon winds which bring water laden clouds with them, bring life for the crops in India. Whenever, the rains are inadequate the human population becomes helpless. Even though rainfall is adequate, water supply becomes a problem in most of the areas in summer. It is more severely experienced in urban societies where the per-capita water requirement are comparatively more and supply sources are limited.

b) Biological Environment: The biological environment form another important surroundings of the human society. The living objects like animals-domesticated and wild, plants, crop plants and wild trees growing in jungles, constitute this environment. Animals that supply milk, wool, meat have been exploited by man right from stoneage for his survival. The wild animals which could not be domesticated are gradually vanishing.

Big jungles with trees and variety of animals and birds are the treasures of nature. They supply fuel, high quality wood, at times medicinal substances and useful raw products like rubber, lakh, gum etc. The trees and jungles are useful in other ways, they not only provide greenery to the earth surface but act as rain attractant. The human society, at many places, experiencing grave situations due to constant desertion of jungles and, therefore, preservation of jungles has become a necessary activity of the Governments and non-governmental organizations.

Microscopic organisms also influence the human life. Their effects on human life are very significant. Some of the organisms cause diseases like Cholera and Malaria. The discovery that diseases are caused by micro organisms has been a great achievement of human beings. Earlier it was presumed that diseases are caused due to acts of demons and accumulation of sins or dissatisfaction of some Gods over the individual. All the micro-organisms are not destructive. There are organisms in the soil which are millions in cubic centimeter of soil. These organisms make the essential elements available to plant roots.

2) Artificial Environment: Every surrounding object which is created by human efforts form the artificial environment. These environments are created so as to suit human needs and desires. The artificial objects such as big buildings, gardens, factories, vehicles are creations of human efforts and are controlled by them. With rapid development of technical know how, the human societies are creating more and more things of their desire either by modifying the natural environment or by establishing foreign objects. The artificial changes have not always resulted favourably. For example, air-pollution has become a problem in many industrial cities of the World. But still to fulfill the upgoing aspirations of increasing population., the environment is bound to become more artificial.

3) Social Environment: Man creates the artificial environment around him in the process of his adjustment to nature. It is not only nature in whose contact he lives, but also among other human beings around him. His relationship with them is another environment which is called social environment. This environment can be splitted into 3 parts; namely - physico- social environment, bio-social environment and psycho-social environment.

a) Physico-social Environment: The physical objects which are prepared by human beings for the use of society come under the physico-social environment. For example, the railway. The train is a physical object created with the co-ordinated efforts of many human groups - the coach factory workers, porters, engine drivers, signal men, managers and so on. It is most useful communication facility in the modern age. The local railways in big cities like Mumbai are called as 'Veins' providing life to the city. It is not, therefore, simply a physical object but a physico-social object. If it is understood that ' railway' is not only a part of physical environment but it also has social significance then we find several socially created physical objects meant for social utilisation like, telephone, radio, Television, stadiums, weapons, machines etc.

b) Bio-social Environment: The plants and animals form the biological environment around us. Just like railways, this environment also has social importance. It is mainly because of human dependence on agriculture that the biological environment has got social implications. Through persistent effort to exploit this environment, man has evolved the high yielding varieties of different crops. These varieties have helped, to a great extent, in fetching more economic gains for the farmers. The crossbreeding of Indian cows with the European breeds has resulted in increasing the milk output, as well as the profit earning capacity of dairies. In India, one can not imagine farming without bullocks. A bullock pair of a farmer is some-thing more for him than only a pair of animals.

c) Psycho-social Environment: The physical and biological environments are formed by nature or by human efforts. A totally different environment which is not seen but felt is the psycho-social environment. In fact when we speak of the social environment, we usually refer to its psycho-social features. This environment exists in the human inter relationships in the society.

The established processes or behaviour in the society and the set ways of thinking and ideologies, which tend to become established in the human minds, contribute to form this environment.

Every individual in the society with his experiences and learning establishes a set of ideas in his mind which are then reflected in his behaviour. These behavioural implications are most influential in the psychological environment.

Culture forms a part of psycho-social environment. Culture is transmitted from generation to generation in many forms, such as traditions, customs, folkways and mores. The traditions are the uniform sanctioned habits of thinking followed in the society. In the olden days when there was little scope for written communication the traditions were preserved and transmitted in the form of songs and phrases. Each community has its own traditions which are influential in conditioning human behaviours. The traditions may be fighting for right cause, for freedom or respecting elder persons.

Customs are the uniform ways of doing things and each custom has a tradition behind it, which is socially approved. This approval imparts a psychological command to those customs over the individual. In the society, customs prevail in all the areas of human life. Birth of new body in the family accompanies a custom of naming the baby ceremoniously. There are countless customs in the areas like religion, hospitality and mourning for the dead.

Culture controls the psycho-social environment by providing approved ways and means of doing things. It, thus indirectly gives stability and order to social inter-relationships. It is because of this stability in the psycho-social environment, that millions of people can live together and perform their roles in the social system.

4) Psychological environment: The psychological environment is not external to man. His values, ideas, instincts, motives and attitudes which are deep rooted in the mind, control his reactions to physical, biological and social environment. In the group behaviour one has to adjust himself because every human individual has some beliefs, attitudes and values of his own. Our conduct, when viewed objectively, is a chain of stimulation and response.

Culture and Development

Culture is the patterns of learned behaviour and the products of behaviour that are shared by the members of a society and are transmitted among them.

i) Culture is the patterns of learned behaviour. It means the individual learns the patterns of culture. A child is not born with culture. He learns it from parents, teachers, playmates and others. The Ferals and Isolate's (the children rared by animals) prove that they did not learn the culture.

ii) Culture is the product of behaviour. The ideas, values and knowledge come to an individual from others which is called non-material culture. The material objects like chair, table, automobile etc., are the products of culture. These are called material culture objects.

iii) Culture is shared by the members of society. The learned behaviour is not the exclusive property of a single individual or group, but it belongs to all the members of society and is shared by a large proportion of them.

iv) Culture is transmitted among the members of a society. Learned behaviour is passed down from one generation to another and is also disseminated among its members. It may be transmitted by word of mouth, by written words, by etchings and paintings on the walls and in various other ways. The new members entering in a society acquire the culture by socialization.

Importance of culture: The understanding of culture is important for the extension worker as he has to deal with the people. Culture can either facilitate or hinder change. An example of culture as a barrier to introduction of new variety of maize is found in North India. Due to higher yields the farmers planted some of their acreage under hybrid maize. However, next year all the farmers rejected the new variety. The explanation is found in the locally accepted evidence of good cooking. The bread made with new variety was yellow in colour, which is identified with careless cooking. The housewives did not wish to be stigmatized as incompetent cooks and refuse to prepare bread from new hybrid maize.

Cultural values may serve as a block to new ideas. Many farmers are reluctant to adopt artificial insemination for their cows. They would increase their farm incomes by selling their dairy bulls, thereby reducing its maintenance cost. The adoption of artificial insemination would also lead to higher quality dairy cattle leading to higher milk yields. However, very few farmers use this practice as they perceive it as unnatural.

Increased importance is attached to the culture in recent years as it helps in formulation and implementation of various development programmes in different areas.

Characteristics of culture:- (1) Culture is learned-Man is born with culture but he learns it through different agencies i.e., parents, religion and school. (2) Culture is transmitted—It is transmitted from generation by its members. (3) Culture is shared —The benefits of culture are shared by its members. (4) Culture is gratifying—It provides the specific ways of satisfying man's biological and social needs. (5) Culture is adoptive—It helps in adjusting to external forces of various kinds. People living in lands of extreme water scarcity or cold or heat adjust their cultural behaviour to adjust with the situations. (6) Culture is integrative —Certain cultural traits may vanish in the current of time but many aspects of culture do not change. People tend to maintain consistency and integration so that society is held together. (7) Culture tends to build ideals for conformity—The culture specifics required patterns of behaviour which are considered ideal patterns and are followed by its members. Thus, culture acts as a means of social control and defines situations, goals, attitudes, values and behaviour patterns for its members.

Patterns of culture—Cultural patterns are the expected modes of behaviour for situations in every-day life., The patterns of culture are in the form of norms which provide guidelines for daily living. These norms are of three types namely; folk-ways, mores and rituals.

(i) *Folkways* are the customary ways of behaving in the society. Persons who do not conform to the folkways may subject to criticism or be considered strange but would not be necessarily penalized. These are expected forms of behaviour but are not rigidly enforced. Greeting elders with 'namaskar' by folded hands or taking off shoes before entering holy places are most common. Folkways almost becomes a habit of the people.

(ii) Mores are the patterns of behaviour considered essential by the society. They are rigidly enforced, and if not followed, the individual is punished by the society. A prohibition against pork is an important more of Muslim society.

(iii) Rituals are the practices and ceremonies followed by the society in dealing with certain situations. In birth, marriage and death in the society certain rituals are observed. These rituals are prescribed by the culture.

Social Interaction

Social Interaction is continuous and reciprocal series of contacts between two or more persons. These contacts may be physical, which means living or travelling together of these persons. These contacts may be symbolic in which the persons use language and gestures for communicating ideas. Communication in some form is essential to social interaction. People will not react to one another without communication.

The social interaction may be of several types. When social interaction assumes a repetitive pattern in a specific direction it is called a social process. These social processes can be broadly classified into two categories namely; the processes of opposition and the processes of unified action. The important processes of opposition are competition and conflict, while the processes of unified action are accomodation, assimilation and co-operation.

Competition: Competition is that form of social interaction in which the individuals strive against each other for the possession or use of some limited material or non material goods. Competition arises from the scarcity of goods, statuses, and services that are widely or universally desired. In the struggle for these scarce goals, competition is usually restrained by tradition, custom, or law. These limiting factors keep it within bounds, and unrestricted competition is seldom found in actual behaviour. The competition which is according to rules and agreed upon principles by the parties is desirable. If rules are violated by the competing parties then it takes the form of unfair competition, which is harmful to the society.

The competition is goal oriented but may be conscious or unconscious. In conscious competition, the competitors are face to face and strive against each other for some objectives. The grocery shop-keeper located in the village know the total amount of trade available in the village. Each shopkeeper tries to attract as many customers as possible by competing with other shop-keepers in the village to get as much of this trade as possible. In other competition the achievement of the goal may mean eliminating others completely. For example, there can be only one winner in the tennis championship.

The unconscious competition occurs when the competing persons have little knowledge of who or where their competitors are. This is not a consequence of the nature of competition but largely the result of limited communication. The farmers in certain areas may try to increase their yields and thus compete with other farmers producing the same product. Competition is thus a cause of social change, in that, it forces persons to adopt new forms of behaviour to attain desired goals.

Conflict: Conflict is a social interaction in which individuals and groups try to achieve their goals by eliminating the opposition. It is an effort to reach the goal but here the emphasis shifts to the opponents, who may attempt to obstruct, injure or even destroy each other. Conflict is, therefore, always conscious and evokes the deepest emotions and strongest passions. On the other hand competition is continuous and impersonal, while conflict is intermittent and personal. For instance, opposing players in a football match may forget that major goal is to win the match and become so angry that they attempt to injure each other. The rules are disregarded and the interaction becomes one of pure conflict. This behaviour may be self-defeating, if the offenders are removed from the tournament and their respective teams penalized.

There are different levels of conflicts. In the psychological conflict an individual fights against his attitudes and values in achieving the goal. This conflict is primarily within the individual or it may be between the individuals and other persons. When people are unable to achieve their life goals, they often become hopeless, discouraged and demoralized. The conflict here is primarily within their own personality and is of mental nature.

The conflict may be between the individuals and small groups or between larger collection of people. The members of all societies have some degree of suspicion or hostility towards other groups. This sentiment that produces this potential hostility is known as ethnocentrism. Ethnocentrism is the tendency to value highly one's own culture as to regard it as superior to other cultures. Sometimes the extreme ethnocentrism leads to conflict between individuals or groups.

Accommodation: Accommodation is the achievement of adjustment between people that permits harmonious acting together in social situations. It is the termination of competing or conflicting relations, between individuals, groups and other human relationship structures. It establishes a state of agreement so that people may work together even though certain differences separate them.

There are different forms of accommodation which help in maintaining equilibrium among the conflicting forces that may break out again into open violence. (a) *Domination* is the extreme form of accommodation when one person gets clear victory over the other. (b) *Compromise* involves mutual concessions in the interest of a particular situation. Here each contending party agrees to make concessions that allow them to reach agreement. (c) In *Conversion* one of the interacting parties accepts the views or actions of the others as its own. This usually happens in case of religious beliefs. (d) In *Tolerance* the contending parties decide to bear with each other, but the basic issue is not eliminated. Each party holds to its position and agrees to live and let live. In this situation the parties do not come to settlement but tolerate behaviour of each other. The tolerance is the process which involves peaceful and harmonious living of people with different cultural background.

It has the idea of co-existence where differences are permitted within a wide range of behaviour.

Assimilation: Assimilation is the complete merging and fusion of two or more bodies into a single common body. This process is analogous to digestion, in which it is said that the food is assimilated. Assimilation in social relationship means that the cultural differences between divergent groupings of people disappear. Finally, both the groups feel, think, and act similarly as they absorb new common traditions, attitudes, and loyalties and consequently take on a new cultural identity. It occurs more readily when the contacts are intimate, personal and face-to-face.

There are two phases of assimilation. In the first phase, the easily noticeable and fairly easy things are acquired. It is called the external phase of assimilation. The examples of this phase are change of language, dress or changing the names. The second phase is the internal phase, which relates to ideas, values and sentiments. This phase takes long time for assimilation.

Co-operation: Co-operation is the form of social interaction in which two or more individuals or groups work together jointly to achieve common goals. In competition also the efforts of the competitors are to achieve the goals. But co-operation and competition is distinguished in terms of means and ends. In co-operation, the individuals work together, while in competition they compete with each other to achieve the goal.

The role of co-operation or mutual aid in social development has been understood long ago. Here the individuals and groups always work together in co-operative action to achieve some material or non material value. It is the joint performance of a task that leads to a desired end.

The emphasis upon goal orientation implies that the participants work together in order to achieve results of common interest. It may be working at the same task such as pulling a cart or it may be doing one part in series of operations, each of which is necessary for achieving a goal. For instance, in the game of football, each member of the team has to play in his position in order to have a game. Most of the achievements in co-operation depend on the working together of the members, doing different co-ordinated tasks. Here the labour is divided so that each can play his role. In short, in co-operation the persons work together towards common end, rather than, individually towards a personal end.

References

1. Anderson, W.A., and Parker, F.B.
Society, Its Organisation and Operation, Affiliated East West Press, Delhi, 1964.
2. Axinn, G.H., and Thorat, S.S.
Modernising World Agriculture, Oxford & IBH Publishing Co., Delhi, 1972.
3. Benor, D., and Harrison, J.Q.
Agricultural Extension—Training and Visit System, World Bank, Washington, 1977.
4. Berlo, D.K.
The Process of Communication. An Introduction to Theory and Practice, Henry Holt and Company, New York, 1960.
5. Busset, G.M.
A Teaching Manual for Educational Psychology, Osmania University, Hyderabad, 1961.
6. Chauhan, S.S.
Advanced Educational Psychology, Vikas Publishing House Pvt. Ltd., Delhi, 1978.
7. Chitambar, J.B.
Introductory Rural Sociology, Wiley Eastern Ltd., Delhi, 1973.
8. Choubey, B.K.
A Handbook of Extension Education, Jyoti Prakashan, Allahabad, 1979.
9. Clark, R.C., and Abraham, R.H.
Administration in Extension, University of Wisconsin, Madison, 1960.
10. Coombs, P.H., and Ahmed, M.
Attacking Rural Poverty, The Johns Hopkins Uni. Press, London, 1974.

11. Dahama, O.P.
Extension and Rural Welfare, Ramprasad and Sons, Agra, 1976.
12. Das, S.S.
General Psychology, Asia Publishing House, Delhi, 1964.
13. Deb, P.C.
Rural Sociology—An Introduction, Kalyani Publishers, Delhi, 1981.
14. Directorate of Extension
Extension Education in Community Development, Govt. of India, Delhi, 1961.
15. Dusenberry, H.L.
An Extension Reference Manual, Department of Extra-mural Studies, Nigeria, 1961.
16. Ensminger, D.
A Guide to Community Development, Govt. of India, Delhi, 1957.
17. Foster, G.M.
Traditional Societies and Technological Change, Allied Publishers Pvt. Ltd., Delhi, 1973.
18. Franco, J.D.
Extension Education and Community Development, Cornell University, New York, 1958.
19. Gangrade, K.D.
Community Organisation in India, Popular Prakashan, Bombay, 1975.
20. Grewal, I.S., and Tamber, R.S.
An Introduction to Extension Education, Punjab Agricultural University, Ludhiana, 1975.
21. Hass, Kenneth, B., and Packer, Harry, Q.
Preparation and Use of Audio-Visual Aids, Prentice Hall, Inc., 1955.
22. Kelsey, L.D., and Hearne, G.C.
Cooperative Extension Work, Comstock Publishing Associates, New York, 1963.
23. Kieffer, R.E., and Cochran, L.W.
Manual of Audio-Visual Techniques, Prentice Hall Inc., 1966.

24. Martin, O.B., and Bliss, R.K.
Spirit and Philosophy of Extension Work. The Foundation of Extension Work, Washington, 1952.

25. Mosher, A.T.
An Introduction to Agricultural Extension, Agriculture Development Council Inc., New York, 1978.

26. Mosher, A.T.
Getting Agricultural Moving, The Agriculture Development Council Inc., New York, 1966.

27. Mosher, A.T.
Extension Teaching in Asian Universities, A Seminar Report, The Agriculture Development Council Inc., New York, 1975.

28. Merrill, F.E.
Society and Culture, Prentice Hall, New Jersey, 1965.

29. Newman, W.H.
Administrative Action, Prentice Hall Inc., England, 1960.

30. Reddy, A.A.
Extension Education, Shree Lakshmi Press, Baptala, 1976.

31. Rogers, E.M.
Social Change in Rural Society, Appleton-Century Crofts, New York, 1960.

32. Rogers, E.M., and Shoemaker, F.F.
Communication of Innovations, The Free Press, New York, 1971.

33. Ross, M.G., and Lappin, D.W.
Community Organisation, Harper & Row, New York, 1955.

34. Sanders, H.C.
Cooperative Extension Service, Prentice Hall, New York, 1967.

35. Sanderson, D.
Rural Sociology and Rural Social Organisation, John Wiley and Sons, New York, 1948.

36. Singh, K.N , Rao, C.S.S., and Sahay, B.N.
Research in Extension Education, Indian Society of Extension Education, Delhi, 1970.

37. Supe, S.V.
Extension Education, Science Publishers, Nagpur, 1973

38. Supe, S.V.
Project Book—Extension Teaching Methods, Deptt. of Agril. Extension, P.K.V., Akola, 1975.

39. Waghmare, S.K.
National Systems of Modernization, Prashant Publishers, Vallabh Vidyanagar, 1980.

40. Wilson, M.C., and Gallup, G.
Extension Teaching Methods, U.S. Department of Agriculture, Washington, 1955.

Index